The Extraordinary A
BENJAMIN SA
Bromsgrove But

The picture on the inside cover is of the British fleet sailing through the Sound, passing Cronenburg Castle at Elsinore. Nelson's division is leading the fleet to the attack on Copenhagen in 1801.

Sources of Information

Unpublished sources.

Cotton Collection in Birmingham Reference Library, vols. 85 and 102.

Boulton and Watt Archives in Birmingham Reference Library.

Sanders Papers in Hereford and Worcester Record Office, B.A. 1218/10, B.A. 1219/9, B.A. 5312/1(i).

Sanders wills in the Public Record Office.

Deeds and Patents relating to Bromsgrove Button Factory in the possession of John Nicholls.

Published Sources.

Bromsgrove Messenger newspaper in Bromsgrove Public Library.

R.B. Prosser, *Birmingham Inventors and Inventions* (1881; reprint 1970).

D. Epstein, *Buttons* (Studio Vista, 1968).

S.L. Luscomb, *The Collectors' Encyclopedia of Buttons* (Crown Publishers, 1967).

R. Southey, *Letters from England* (1807; reprint, A. Sutton, 1984).

G.K. Stanton, *Rambles and Researches Among Worcestershire Churches* (Bromsgrove, 1884).

W.G. Leadbetter, *The Story of Bromsgrove* (1946).

J. Bentley, *History, Guide and Directory of Worcestershire* (1841).

G.C. Allen, *The Industrial Development of Birmingham and the Black Country* (1929; reprint 1966).

A. Richards et al., *Bygone Bromsgrove* (Bromsgrove Society, 1981).

A. & S. Richards, *Picture Book of Bygone Bromsgrove* (Bromsgrove Society, 1983).

P.D. Curtin, *The Image of Africa, 1780–1850* (Wisconsin, 1964). (For information on yellow fever.)

W. Hutton, *An History of Birmingham* (3rd. edition, 1795).

F. Braudel, *Capitalism and Material Life, 1400–1800* (Fontana, 1974).

R. Perkins, *Gunfire in Barbary: 1816 Campaign in Algiers* (K. Mason, 1982).

P. Mathias, *The First Industrial Nation* (Methuen, 1969).

A. Bryant, *The Years of Victory, 1802–1812* (Collins, 1944).

W. Miller, *A New History of the United States* (Paladin, 1970).

O. Warner, *Nelson and the Age of Fighting Sail* (Cassell, 1963).

P. Hughes & N. Molyneux, *Worcester Streets: Friar Street* (1984).

Fairbairn, *Book of Crests* (1892).

G. E. Evans, *The Horse in the Furrow* (Faber, 1960).

The Extraordinary Adventures of Benjamin Sanders Buttonmaker of Bromsgrove

His personal account put into historical perspective

by

Alan Richards

published by

The Bromsgrove Society

TO

John H. Nicholls.

First published as a Special Limited Edition in 1984.

ISBN 0 9509471 2 1

Printed in England by Avon Litho, Stratford-upon-Avon.

Contents

Foreword.

John Nicholls really began this book when he enquired, almost casually, if I would like to read a memoir written by the founder of his firm, Benjamin Sanders, in 1833. He had acquired a typescript of this memoir in about 1950, after the original memoir, in Benjamin Sanders's own handwriting, had lain forgotten in a lawyer's office for many years. One of the last descendants of the Sanders family in Bromsgrove, Mr. Sanders of Lion House, Ednall Lane, secretary of the Jewellers' Association of Birmingham, had had the memoir copied and had circulated a few copies amongst his friends. It is believed that he then sent the original manuscript to a member of the Sanders family in the U.S.A.

The memoir was first printed in the Bromsgrove Society Newletter, 1983 – 1984, in serial form, and aroused such interest that John Foster asked me to set the memoir in its historical background, so that it could be published by the Society. I welcomed the opportunity to put this gem of a record in its historical setting, because it is a good example of the primary stuff of history. There is an immediacy and intimacy about memoirs, letters and diaries which make history come alive.

First and foremost Benjamin Sanders's memoir reveals a good deal about his character: his strong religious faith, resilience, kindliness, diligence and inventive genius, and also his anger and despair at his worst moments. His story is an inspiring one of major setbacks being overcome. Benjamin Sanders, however, not only wrote a fascinating, short biography, but also a valuable record of business history. His invention of 1813 has been rightly called the most important single invention of the button industry. Unfortunately the early business records of his firm in Bromsgrove were destroyed in the fire at the Button Factory in 1915.

His memoir is also a valuable primary source of history for the light it throws on a grim and little known episode of the Napoleonic Wars, the British invasion of Denmark, and the siege and bombardment of

Copenhagen in 1807. As an eyewitness of many of the events of this episode, he did not see it from a narrow nationalistic point of view, but from the unusual viewpoint of one who suffered from the actions of his own countrymen. As a result, he understood the hostile Danish attitudes to Britain and to himself at the end of the war. He also made some strongly critical comments on British policy during the Napoleonic Wars, and on the behaviour of some powerful people.

All the original spelling and punctuation of the memoir has been kept, and my additions have been put into different type. The chapter headings have been added by me, but written in the style of novels in Benjamin Sanders's own time. The portraits of Benjamin Sanders and his wife are from original oil paintings in the possession of Dr. P. Gurrey, one of their descendants.

No footnotes have been provided, but the sources of information are given in the bibliography. John Foster kindly read through the draft and saved me from several errors. Richard Wilday has used his customary skill in producing the photographic prints for the book. Margaret Cooper, Tim Brotherton and Peter Woollacott provided several vital pictures and information. Norman Neasom A.R.S.W. designed the title page and the map of Bromsgrove's mills in splendid period style. Finally my wife acted once again as my typist and helpmate.

Introduction

Fashions in the 1780's and 1790's. 'The Bath Beau and the Country Beau', C.1788 – 1790. Artist: Thomas Rowlandson. Note the many buttons on coats, pockets, cuffs, waistcoats and breeches.

As for myself, I take great displeasure
In tales of those who once knew wealth and leisure
And then are felled by some unlucky hit.
But it's a joy to hear the opposite,
For instance tales of men of low estate
Who climb aloft and growing fortunate
Remain secure in their prosperity;
That is delightful as it seems to me
And is a proper sort of tale to tell.

Chaucer, "Canterbury Tales".

Geoffrey Chaucer was once the Keeper of Feckenham Forest in which lay the royal manor of Bromsgrove, and he would certainly have taken pleasure in the story of Benjamin Sanders, whose Button Factory in Bromsgrove raised him to fame and fortune. Benjamin Sanders's story is that of making, losing and regaining his fortune, and his experiences of swindlers, pirates, hostile French ships, Red Indians, yellow fever, plundering soldiers, and finally of imprisonment, despair and near death during the siege of Copenhagen in 1807. He had thirteen narrow escapes from death before he reached the age of forty-five. His ingenious button inventions and business sense enabled him to establish successful businesses in places as wide apart as London, New York, Laminburg, Copenhagen, Birmingham and Bromsgrove. He manufactured buttons in London, New York, Birmingham and most successfully in Bromsgrove; also leather in Laminburg and silk in Copenhagen. Midway in his career, his business and fortune in Denmark were destroyed during the Napoleonic Wars, and he had to rebuild his fortune from scratch at the age of forty-five. Sadly his beautiful country house in Denmark, ironically named "Peaceful Retirement", was in the front line during the British invasion of Denmark and was destroyed by British soldiers, who stabled their horses in its best rooms, burned all his furniture as firewood, and even carried off the soil from his gardens.

Benjamin Sanders saw some of the effects of three major revolutions in his lifetime, the American Revolution, the French Revolution and the Industrial Revolution. His England was the England of James Watt and Nelson; his Europe was that of Robespierre and Napoleon; his America was that of George Washington and Thomas Jefferson. During the lifetime of Benjamin Sanders, Britain became the world's first industrial nation, and, as one of the first factory owners, he helped to begin a new economic era. In the 1780's, when he was in his twenties, Britain took off industrially, and just before his death, the Great Exhibition of 1851 showed off Britain's industrial might. While Benjamin Sanders was still a young man, Mathew Boulton, James Watt and Richard Arkwright were laying the foundations for the new age of machines, steam power and factories.

Bromsgrove had been a centre for the manufacture of woollen cloth since the Middle Ages, and was well to the fore in adopting some of the new spinning machines and steam power of the Industrial Revolution. Two of the earliest cotton spinning factories in England were established in Bromsgrove at the end of the eighteenth century: the Cotton Mill in Watt Close and Sidemoor Mill (the Button Factory later). One of Richard Arkwright's spinning machines or water frames, with nine hundred and sixty spindles was installed in the Cotton Mill in Watt Close. A steam engine was installed in Sidemoor Mill at the end of the eighteenth century by Richard Collett, a manufacturer of linen cloth, who lived at Cherry Orchard Farm. This steam engine was almost certainly built by James Watt in the Soho Works of Boulton and Watt in Handsworth, Birmingham.

Some of the biggest industrial fortunes made in Birmingham in the eighteenth century were founded on the manufacture of buttons. Mathew Boulton was a large scale manufacturer of cut steel buttons by the mid-eighteenth century in his Soho Works, before he became James Watt's partner in the manufacture of steam engines. John Taylor was described as Birmingham's largest manufacturer in 1766, and he became very rich after introducing many improvements in gilt, plated and lacquered buttons. William Hutton, Birmingham's historian in the eighteenth century, called John Taylor, "the Shakespeare or the Newton of his time." Taylor's techniques and other Birmingham methods of casting and making hollow pewter and tin buttons, made the production of metal buttons cheaper, and they reached a wider market.

English metal buttons were moulded or stamped from pewter, silver, brass and copper and the designs on them were often miniature works of art. Pewter buttons were scorned by the upper classes in the eighteenth century, but were widely used by poorer people. There was a strong connection between the jewellery business and button manufacture at first, as silversmiths and jewellers cast and moulded many of the more expensive buttons. Sparkling gilt buttons were first manufactured in Birmingham at the end of the eighteenth century; these were brass buttons thinly coated with a wash of gold.

Benjamin Sanders was born in the age of magnificent buttons, which increased in size, number and variety on the dress of gentlemen during the eighteenth century. Gentlemen wore large buttons on their tailcoats, multi-coloured buttons on their waistcoats, buttons on the knees of their buckskin breeches, as well as buttons on their gaiters. English fashion copied the French male mania for lavish and extravagant buttons which made well dressed men into walking picture galleries. The Comte d'Artois wore a set of diamond buttons, in each of which was set a miniature watch. Fabric buttons were hand embroidered in multi-coloured silks and fetched high prices. Louis XV had his own button-maker to ensure the perfection of his buttons. Birmingham's button business began in the 1660's with Birmingham's button-makers copying French buttons. Metal buttons began to replace the expensive fabric buttons in the early eighteenth century. The newer fashion of narrower, closer fitting garments for men, and the growing popularity of the double-breasted style demanded more buttons by the mid-eighteenth century.

By 1800 cloth-covered buttons were all the rage in England, and large metal buttons had gone out of fashion. R. Southey pictured a Spaniard arriving in Engand in 1800 wearing the wrong kind of buttons for English fashion, thus betraying that he was a foreigner: "I fancied my figure was quite English in my pantaloons of broad-striped fustian, and large coat buttons of cut steel; but it seems that although they are certainly of genuine English manufacture, they were manufactured only for foreign sale. Tomorrow my buttons will be covered, and my toes squared, and I shall be in no danger of being called Frenchman in the streets."

Benjamin Sanders's invention of a method of making buttons by machinery was a response to this great demand for cloth-covered buttons. His invention was rightly called the most important single invention in the button industry. He was one of those comparatively rare people who was both an inventor and a successful industrialist. He had the qualities which both of these types of people needed, an interest in innovation, an appreciation of future possibilities, an above average amount of energy, organising ability and a good business sense. Individual entrepreneurs, like Benjamin Sanders, played a great part in the growth of industry and have been called by P. Mathias "the shock troops of economic change." On these grounds he deserved to be more widely known as one of the pioneers of the Industrial Revolution.

Chapter I

In which Benjamin Sanders is apprenticed to a tailor in Worcester; seeks his fortune in London and falls in love with Phoebe.

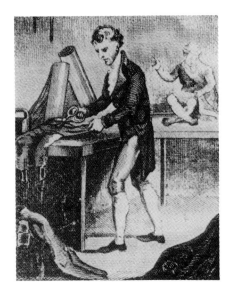

A tailor from a book of trades of 1811.

*A linen draper
from a book of trades of 1824.*

Chapter I

By the persuasion of friends who are acquainted with the various changes of fortune that have attended me and my family through life, and who consider it a duty I owe to society to communicate the results of my experience, I am induced (being now of the age of seventy years) to give my readers the history of my life; with some hope that, if candidly perused, the relation may tend both to amuse and instruct them.

In my earliest days I was considered to possess an ingenious disposition; and my father, a very exemplary character, lost no opportunity of instilling into my youthful mind those precepts that might contribute to my present and future welfare: he and William Shenstone, the poet of the Leasowes, were first cousins, and passed their early school days together at Hales Owen. As my mind expanded I became more and more sensible of the work of my father, and still increased in my affectionate attachment to him. When I was eight years old he placed me under the Rev. Mr. Taylor, of Worcester, in which city we resided, and where I was born. In a very few weeks I took a great dislike to my preceptor, who was so morose a man that I could scarcely consider him possessed of human feelings. Fortunately for me I was transferred to a gentleman of the most opposite disposition; this was Dr. Roberts, a truly amiable man. Under his instructions I found myself exceedingly happy; and have, I thank God, reaped from them a profitable harvest.

My father's prospects about this time became clouded, he having a large family, and he felt anxious as to my settlement in life. He had two sisters in the town of Bromsgrove, one of whom had a son in excellent business as a linen and woollen draper; and my father thought that by apprenticing me to Mr. Lingham, a person in the trade, I might possibly when out of my time succeed to my cousin's business. Accordingly I was taken from school and apprenticed, sixty pounds being paid to him as premium. At the expiration of half a year of my servitude, I conceived a dislike to passing my time in the draper's shop, and took a great fancy to the tailor's cutting-room, which seemed to afford greater scope to what ingenuity

I possessed. I was indulged in this preference; and in four years became by diligent application, a competent and excellent workman, and far superior to my instructors. But notwithstanding the progress I had made, I still felt a dissatisfaction I could not account for. The time passed tediously, particularly the last two years of my apprenticeship, my mind being bent towards London, and I no sooner became free than I determined to gratify my inclination.

With my father's blessing and instructions, and the concurrence of all friends, I took my departure accompanied by my brother, who was well acquainted with London. He very soon found a situation to suit me; having paid a premium to a master tailor, who had a very genteel connection in business, to instruct me in his cutting-room.

When this matter was settled, we paid a visit to another brother, who was well situated, having married a widow whose relations lived respectably in Somersetshire. This brother's wife had two sisters in town, one married, the other single. We went one afternoon, by appointment, to take tea with them, and found in the parlour two ladies, one of whom was Mrs. Smart, the married sister just mentioned, and the other was a most accomplished old lady, named Lindesay, who will be mentioned hereafter. In a little time came in a young lady who seemed to look favourably on me, and I certainly admired her. Our mutual feeling I consider a blessing from heaven; we were struck at once with an impulse of deep regard for each other, which has lasted without intermission from that time to this.

The next day was that appointed for the departure of the brother who had accompanied me to London. We loved each other tenderly, and the loss of his society produced in me a great depression of spirits. He encouraged me as well as he could, by telling me how much better I was situated than most young men, as his connections in London were now become mine — "Besides (said he) you will still have a brother in town who will always be glad to see you." But, alas! I found the case otherwise; for my London brother was too religious to expect any good to come of my visits.

My thoughts, when my other brother had returned to the country, turned to the business of my situation, in which I gave satisfaction. I had, however, been but a little time with my employer when I found he was not so punctual in business as he should have been, punctuality being a quality which all tradesmen should particularly practise. By degrees I became intimate with all my London brother's acqaintances and was very kindly received by them, particularly by the sister of his wife, whom I was in the habit of visiting every evening. I would here wish to give some account of Mrs. Lindesay, mentioned above. She was first cousin to Archdeacon Congreve, whose virtuous principles make him an ornament to mankind. Mrs. Lindesay was the daughter of Governor Congreve but lived under the fostering care of the Archdeacon. Mrs. Smart (my wife's sister), being a very sensible clever woman, was engaged by Mrs. Lindesay as housekeeper to the Archdeacon. Mrs. Smart's conduct gained her universal esteem in the family, and gained Mrs. Lindesay's affections. Mrs. Lindesay was the widow of Captain Lindesay, who was unfortunately wounded at the battle of Bunker's Hill, in the unhappy War in North America. The good Archdeacon dying, left all his effects to Mrs. Lindesay, whose affections being settled on Mrs. Smart, she came and lived with her on the footing of a most tender sister. There I found this most happy family whom I loved, and was as sincerely beloved by.

This was a most blissful period of my life; but alas, this worldly happiness was of short duration; Mrs. Smart received a letter from Somersetshire, from an old aunt, desiring her to send her sister Phoebe down to nurse her in her illness. My readers who are blessed with tender feelings can conceive the parting of two such congenial souls; but part we did; our last look on each other confirmed our love. To console me, Mrs. Lindesay and Mrs. Smart proposed I should lodge in the same house with them during the absence of the one Smart esteemed. This was well and sensibly managed, and as l was a young man, perhaps prevented consequences that might have embittered my feelings during my future life. I was naturally fond of good company, therefore, I could not be more agreeably situated. In the evenings Mrs. Lindesay would often entertain me with singular accounts of the Archdeacon's benevolence; one among the many was the circumstance that follows. At a certain time, when the servant had to lock up the plate, there was a considerable quantity missing, to the great consternation of all the family, particularly the servants; at last the thief was found to be the under cook, as the butler found concealed in her box all the missing plate. This occasioned great joy among the servants; transportation was pronounced to a certainty, but such was not the case. The Archdeacon ordered her and all the servants into his presence, where his admonition was very impressive; he forgave the woman, and allowed her a weekly maintenance. I have often pondered on the Archdeacon's virtues, and the more I have thought on them, the more I esteemed the man. What a Christian example was here to clergymen in general.

I must now turn to my employer, whose propensities I could no longer endure; his affairs grew worse and worse, until he was reduced to a state of bankruptcy. Now this affected me as well as his unfortunate family, as I had to look for another employer. A Mr. Lingham, a son of the person I served my apprenticeship to, had gone into business in the Strand; he had a young man of the name of Richards with him as clerk. Mr. Richards and myself were always on exceeding good terms; being townsmen, we were happy in seeing each other in London. He was a young man of talent, and exceeding good accomplishments. We both knew Mr. Lingham in his juvenile days to be inclined to principles not very creditable; but as he was in good business, my friend was of opinion that he had now arrived at the age of discretion, and that if I would take to the cutting-room department we should all be doing well. It suited me certainly, at this junction of my affairs to do so, and we went on exceedingly well for some time, but Mr. Lingham relapsed into all his natural propensities, which threw my friend Richards and myself into unspeakable sorrow and confusion. We found he had suddenly launched himself into the character of the basest villian. The reader will excuse me for not giving any further details of this unfortunate man, and turning to a more worthy character. My friend Richards was a man seemingly born for the stage, having a good figure, a fine melodious voice, a thorough knowledge of music, and his parents had bestowed on him an excellent education. He was a great favourite at Bristol many years, and by his prudence acquired some considerable property; he left the stage, and purchased a commission in the army for his brother and himself, and both got killed at the battle of Corunna, in Spain (1809).

I shall now proceed with my faithful narrative. I pass now from St. James's church, Piccadilly, with my wife under my arm, we walked home, and found in our friends' faces that satisfaction which is mostly seen on such occasions. I soon began to commence business; one of my lucky customers was a gentleman from Worcester whom I met in Pall Mall; he, for my father's sake, employed and recommended me, desiring me to call on him at Knightsbridge, and measure him for his sheriff's suit of clothes, he being chosen sheriff for the county. This order being executed, gave great satisfaction, and got me further recommendation. I was always very particular in being punctual which example I most strenuously recommend to all tradesmen, and most earnestly to be careful to look to what they owe. The tailor's business is a very perplexing one, and requires vast care to arrive at respectability. I have had to establish business on three different foundations, all of them very reputable. I found it a very good maxim to provide for my acceptances, and if I saw clearly I could spare money when I went to my draper's,

I gave it them to set against my account; a little at a time occasionally repeated, amounted to a great deal, and made my account light at the year's end. I know men that have launched into extravagances, and spent what should have been paid to their tradesmen who have given them credit. Price and vanity are great enemies to mankind. Men that I have been acquainted with have wretchedly suffered them to wither their substance and render their unfortunate situation irretrievable. I have had much experience and I affirm that if people would adhere to the example I have set, they would be certain of prosperity in this world, and happiness in the next.

Benjamin Sanders was born in Worcester in 1763 into what was probably an old Worcestershire family, for he had relatives in Bromsgrove and Halesowen. He does not mention his father's trade in his memoirs, but his cousin, James Wilkinson, had an excellent business in Bromsgrove as a linen and woollen draper. His father was first cousin to William Shenstone the poet (1714-1763), a native of Halesowen, who created beautiful walks in the grounds of his house at Leasowes, one and a half miles to the north-east of Halesowen. Benjamin Sanders's uncle was heir-at-law to William Shenstone. It is probable that Benjamin Sanders's father was a member of the Sanders family which owned an extensive business as woollen drapers and mercers in Worcester for about one hundred and fifty years, between c.1700 and c.1850. The business of the Sanders family in Worcester was located in Friar Street on the corner with Lich Street. Photographs of this building, now demolished, show the name Sanders and a date, 1712, embossed on the corner of the building. Benjamin Sanders's father clearly hoped that his son would inherit the flourishing linen and woollen draper's business in Bromsgrove from his cousin, James Wilkinson. When he was about twelve years old, he was taken away from school to be apprenticed for seven years to a draper and tailor in Worcester, Mr. Lingham.

After moving to London in about 1782, and becoming a tailor in a shop in the Strand belonging to Mr. Lingham (junior), he became very friendly with Mr. Richards, a clerk in the same business. Mr. Richards was later killed in the battle of Corunna in 1809, during the Peninsula War. This battle took place in north-western Spain, after an English army, commanded by Sir John Moore, had made a desperate hit-and-run attack on the French, followed by a retreat to Corunna, where they were taken off by the British navy. Sir John Moore was also killed in this battle.

Chapter II

In which Benjamin is cheated by a swindler, but is saved by a benevolent banker.

London in 1819. St. Martin's-le-Grand, home of the General Post Office, with St. Paul's in the background.

Chapter II.

My business prospered, and I was doing well; but at a certain period I met with a singular circumstance. I had a woollen draper whom I had done business with upwards of two years (a Mr. F. Senr.) whose son conducted the business; he was a very clever young man, about my own age; we became much acquainted. He came to me one day and asked if I would do his father the favour to accept a bill, and his father would pay it when it became due; it was for a considerable amount. I made some hesitation, but through the persuasion of his son I accepted the bill, payable at two months. I was going on business one morning, when on my way I met the son, who informed me his father had made a very advantageous purchase and immediate payment was required; if I had any money in the house, and I would accommodate his father, the money would soon be returned. I had so much confidence that I told him to go to my wife, and desire her to give him so much out of my cash drawer, I being in haste at that time could not go back with him. At my return my wife expostulated with me to an extent that alarmed me. Women, I have sometimes found to be possessed of more penetration than men, and it proved particularly so in my wife's fears on the above occasion. Mr. F. forfeited his word and honour in the first place, by not returning at the time appointed the money his son received from my wife. I found my wife's mind filled with apprehensions that utter ruin must be the consequence, and her fears were verified when the day arrived. Three days before the day of payment, I went to Mr. F. and gave him the notice from the banker; he told me he could not take up the bill. I asked him for the money his son got from my wife; even this he refused, saying, "I dare say you can take up the bill, I assure you it is out of my power". I left him with indignation. His son came after me, and made mean proposals to me, such as pawning his father's property; I left him with as much contempt as I left his father.

I had now to return home to my wife, and I satisfied her that I had hopes of collecting money sufficient to take up the bill. There was no time to be lost; I exerted myself to the utmost of my power, but could not accomplish the means. I came home in a fit of despair, and threw myself down on a sofa; through fatigue and distress of mind I dropped off and slept about an hour. When I awoke I found myself refreshed; I was struck with the thought that I would make my case known to the banker who held the bill. This notion was met with the approval of my wife, and I set out to the banker's, near the Mansion House. In going along my heart began to fail, knowing how difficult it was to get an interview with gentlemen in the situation of bankers; but my resolution became more and more strengthened.

I at length entered the first apartment of the banking-house, where I informed them I had particular business with one of the principals of the house. They took an observation of me, and very politely conducted me into the further apartment. The gentleman in that apartment pressed me to communicate my business to them. I informed them it was with one of the firm personally. Finding me inflexible, they with great politeness conducted me upstairs where I remained solus some time, not knowing whether to jump out of the window or run down stairs into the street. At length this reverie was put a period to by the opening of a door, when a very gentlemanly looking person approached in a very polite manner, saying, "Sir, I am given to understand you have business of consequence with me". "Yes, Sir, (I replied) I am a young tradesman," — "Pooh, pooh, pooh", and he was going to ring the bell. My expectation was that I should be kicked down-stairs. I told him I came here, being confident of seeing a gentleman, and hoped he would have the goodness and patience to hear what I had to communicate. He turned to me with a more favourable aspect; after a little conversation, he politely moved a chair, and invited me to sit down. I asked him if a Mr. F. did not have his bills discounted at his house; he said he did, he believed. Then I told him the whole matter that my readers are already acquainted with. I informed him I had never had a bill dishonoured in my life, though I had paid many bills into his house, but the one in question. In answer he said, "Stay here, and in a little time I shall return". He was away about half an hour, when he returned with the bill in his hand, saying, "Sir, I have taken up the bill myself, and you can pay it at your own convenience". There is nothing so noble as an act of benevolence. I gratefully withdrew, and he followed me to the door with marks of great satisfaction in his countenance. On going down-stairs, I found I had forgot that I had part of the money for the bill in my pocket. I immediately returned and just tapped at the inner door; when I was admitted I informed him of the cause of my return, and presented him the money. He took my bill and put this money with it, and returned the whole into his desk, saying, "Young man, be sure not to put yourself to any inconvenience in taking up the bill". He politely waited on me to the door again, and I passed the gentlemen in the lower department like a man of great consequence. In going home I could scarcely believe matters so favourable, and I returned to my wife with smiling satisfaction. I now applied my exertions to liquidate the bill, which I did in two payments, much sooner than I or the banker expected.

I was always after admitted to this gentleman without ceremony; the last payment I had a good deal of conversation with him; he gave me the bill, and desired me to call on him in the following week, which I punctually did. When I called, he behaved to me like a father, expressing his good opinion of me in a most kind and affable manner. He said he should like to employ me as his tailor, but his old tailor was living, who made his first infant suit of clothes, and he had been in his employ ever since; he assured me, if anything should happen to his old tailor, he would employ me, and he should recommend me whenever he had an opportunity, and desiring me to wait on Dr. Creighton in Leicester-fields. I waited on Dr. Creighton accordingly, and found him a complete gentleman in manner. I found my friend the banker had mentioned the mode in which I gained his friendship.

Chapter III

In which his extraordinary invention, the "ventilator", for men's breeches, brings laughter to London society, but his quarrel with a nobleman ruins him.

Buying Leather Breeches — Previous to our Journey. (1784) Artist: T. Rowlandson.

Chapter III.

While he was still in his twenties, Benjamin Sanders showed his inventive abilities by making a 'ventilator' or circular spring, which he fitted into the seats of tight breeches. The spring enabled men to bend and dance more comfortably. This invention became a best seller for a short time and made him one of the most fashionable tailors in London. One of his aristocratic customers promised to recommend him to the Prince of Wales, the highest commendation for any tailor.

The fashion of wearing very tight-fitting leather breeches fastened with buttons was graphically described by Robert Southey at the end of the eighteenth century: "...everybody wore leathern breeches, which were made so tight that it was a good half-hour's work to get them on the first time. The maker was obliged to assist at this operation:— observe, this personage is not called a tailor, but a maker of breeches — tailors are considered as an inferior class, and never meddle with leather. When a gentleman was in labour of a new pair of leathern breeches, all his strength was required to force himself into them and all the assistant operators to draw them on: when it was nearly accomplished, the maker put his hands between the patient's legs, closed them, and bade him sit on them like a saddle, and kick out one leg at a time, as if swimming. They could not be buttoned without the help of an instrument. Of course they fitted like another skin; but woe to him who was caught in the rain in them! — it was like plucking a skin off to get out of them."

It was important to have the right number of buttons on these breeches and on other garments and the latest patterns of buttons in order to be in fashion. Southey gave one of the best summaries of the caprice of fashion at the end of the eighteenth century:—

"The shoes — I am not going back beyond a score of years in any of these instances — were made to a point in our unnatural method; they were then rounded, then squared, lastly made right and left like gloves to fit the feet. At one time the waistcoat was so long as to make the wearer seem all body; at another time so short that he was all limbs. The skirts of the coat were now cut away so as almost to leave all behind bare as a baboon, and now brought forward to meet over the thigh like a petticoat. Now the cape was laid flat upon the shoulders, now it stood up straight and stiff like an implement of torture, now was rounded off like a cable. Formerly the half-boot was laced: the first improvement was to draw it on like a whole-boot; it was then discovered that a band at the back was better than a seam, and that a silken tassel in front would be highly ornamental, and no doubt of essential use. By this time the half-boot was grown to the size of the whole one. The Austrians, as they were called, yielded to the Hessians, which having the seams on each side instead of down the back were more expensive and therefore more fashionable. Then came an invention for wrinkling the leather upon the instep into round folds, which were of singular utility in retaining the dirt and baffling the shoe-black. At length a superior genius having arisen among boot-makers, the wheel went completely round, and at this present time every body must be seen in a pair of whole-boots of this great man's making.

I asked my tailor one day, who is a sensible man in his way, who invented the fashions. "Why, sir," said he, "I believe it is the young gentlemen who walk in Bond-street. They come to me, and give me orders for a new cut, and perhaps it takes, and perhaps it does not. It is all fancy, you know sir." This street serves as a Prado or Alameda for all the fops of rank, and happy is he who gets the start in a new cut; in the fall of a cape, the shape of a sleeve, or the pattern of a button. This emulation produces many abortive attempts, and it is amusing to see the innovations which are daily hazarded without ever attaining to the dignity of a fashion.

My tailor tells me I must have pantaloons of a reddish cast, "All on the reds now, sir!" and reddish accordingly they are, in due conformity to his prescription. It is even regulated whether the coat shall be worn open or buttoned, and if buttoned, whether by one button or two, and by which. Sometimes a cane is to be carried in the hand, sometimes a club, sometimes a common twig; at present the more deformed and crooked in its growth the better At one time every man walked the streets with his hands in his coat pocket. The length of the neck-handkerchief, the shape, the mode of tying it, must all be in the mode. There is a professor in the famous Bond-street, who, in lessons at half-a-guinea, instructs gentlemen in the art of tying their neck-handkerchiefs in the newest and most approved style."

There was a lot of truth in a well-known text of the eighteenth century,

"The tailors have more trouble inventing than sewing." Fortunately Benjamin Sanders had no trouble inventing and in addition to his buttons and 'ventilator', he was the first to suggest the use of silk nap as a substitute for the beaver, then used in hats, and also he invented an improved form of joint for bedsteads.

By a little ingenuity I made various inventions in business, one in particular brought me into publicity. Clothes at that time being worn exceedingly tight, and breeches particularly, I found much inconvenience complained of, which I thought I could remedy by a circular spring behind, which gave ease in dancing and exercise. By this, and punctuality in business, I got a very genteel connexion. One morning two gentlemen called, and one of them particularly requested me to attend him next morning, and wrote his address in my book, "Montague, Upper Harley Street". They were two exceedingly fine well grown young gentlemen. I went according to order, and found I must address him as his lordship. I took his lordship's order, and punctually executed it, to his great satisfaction. In a short time he came with the same gentleman, who desired me to wait on him. This was Sir Richard Beddingfield. Their gentlemanly manner gave me great pleasure in executing their orders; they became my favourite customers, particularly Lord Montague, who recommended me to more of the young nobility. My circular spring did wonders for me, and far exceeded my expectations.

There was a gentleman of the name of Darrell, a Director of the East India Company, who was a very good customer, exceeding partial to me. I waited on him one morning with some clothes, when he informed me the Prince of Wales would dine with him that day, and if an opportunity should occur, he would recommend me to His Royal Highness. This gentleman took me into a room to show me a set of harness for six or more horses, which harness he was going to send to his son in India. I was amazed at its elegance and splendour; I never saw anything of the kind so magnificent. We now went into his dressing-room, where he tried his clothes to see all was perfect to dress in for dinner, a magnificent one no doubt. He had put on all his clothes but his coat, when he rang the bell for his valet, whom he ordered to request Mrs. Darrell to come into his dressing-room. In came Mrs. Darrell, whom I never saw before, a most elegant lady. She required to know what he wanted with her. "My dear, (said he) this is Mr. Sanders, the most punctual tradesman I ever employed, and he is the inventor of the much admired spring smallclothes," at the same time turning about, and putting himself in all postures. She was very attentive in looking on my rotatory invention; it did its duty perfectly. He stooped down sufficiently low to pick anything from the ground, then raised himself, saying, "My dear, is it not a clever thing — what is your opinion?" — "My opinion my dear, is that it looks like a ventilator", bursting out in an extreme fit of laughter, casting her eyes on me, and running out of the room. I could not contain myself, the idea struck me so forcibly, that I could not refrain from a fit of laughter; so much so that I was ashamed. Mr. Darrell looked at me with a very smiling good natured countenance; he was a most amiable man. After my apology for my rudeness, and the surprise had dissipated, he said to me, "Mr. Sanders, it is very wonderful the construction women often put upon things; he considered a little, and then burst out into an immoderate fit of laughter himself, and my readers are at liberty to laugh too, if they can figure to themselves this interview with the good Mr. Darrell and his lady. I believe this laughing proceeded like a contagion; it got among the upper circles, where laughing became general on this important ventilator, for I found the news flew to all comers of the west end of the town.

I was astonished, however, some time after, at finding a great falling off in the popularity of my ventilator, as the lady called it, but it got me a very genteel connexion, and I went on in business for some time very smoothly, but unfortunately a circumstance happened that put a period to my prosperity in London.

I was treated very ill by a young nobleman, a very good customer; I came to him, I confess, a quarter of an hour after he expected, and he gave me such language as disgusted me. I made some remark that I did not require nor deserve such language from any gentleman much less a nobleman. His passion on this rose to such a pitch, that he was going to give me chastisement, but I finished this by putting a stop to his lordship's intention. This was a matter which operated against me, he having such influence among my customers that I soon found I was in danger of losing my business. I was thus in a very disagreeable situation. Next night Lord Montague drove to my house, desiring me to come to him by six o'clock next morning. I pretty well knew by his lordship's manner he was displeased with me. I had a restless night, and no sleep. I rose at five o'clock, and dressed myself genteely, as usual, and got to his lordship's door a quarter before the time; I had, therefore, a little space to prepare myself for the interview. I consoled myself by thinking his lordship would not be displeased with me when I explained to him my situation. His valet came to me, saying I must go into his lordship's bed-room. I knocked at the door, his lordship told me to come in; he sat up in his bed, pushed the curtain violently back, saying "Sanders, come here, and sit down by my bedside". His lordship began by telling me of my conduct towards the nobleman I have mentioned. I began then to make my defence, but he would not hear it, and expressed himself in such terms, that I found it impossible to make any impression on his lordship in my favour, with all my entreaties, and telling his lordship that if he and Sir R. Beddingfield would stay by me, I cared not if I was divested of all my other customers; and that it was from pure respect that I took the liberty of soliciting. All this was of no avail, his lordship was inflexible, but said in a very kind manner, "Sanders, you are a clever young man; I would advise you to travel and see the world; Sir Richard and myself are going abroad; have you any intention to travel?" I answered his lordship in the affirmative. "What part of the world should you like?" I told his lordship America. "Well, (said his lordship) in the name of God, do so." He then desired me to send in his account.

Benjamin Sanders was not the only inventor who thought along the lines of introducing a ventilator into men's tight-fitting breeches. John Tomkins of Woodstock also invented some "patent ventilating breeches" and he advertised them in an eighteenth century newspaper:—

> John Tomkins of Woodstock, Leather-cutter, having philosophically considered the causes of galling in riding, and found it to proceed merely from heat, has after long study, contrived leather breeches with valves so adapted as to suffer air to pass in freely; but to let none pass out. This having a double advantage both in point of coolness and sweetness. He hopes this will meet with the approbation of all gentlemen, who ride during the hot weather.
> NB: Allowance made to postillions and out-riders who take a number.

Just as Benjamin Sanders was becoming a fashionable and successful tailor in London, he suffered his first major setback, when he quarrelled with this unpleasant young nobleman. It was enough, in those days, to ruin his business with the aristocracy. At the age of twenty-nine, with a young wife and two young children, both under the age of five, he decided to seek his fortune in America.

Chapter IV

Containing his meeting with the Rev. George Parker, who was later foully murdered at Oddingley, near Droitwich, and an account of the Worcestershire murders.

Top: picture: The murder of Rev. G. Parker in 1806.
Middle picture: The murder of R. Hemming in 1806.
Bottom picture: The discovery of R. Hemming's skeleton complete with a carpenter's rule in 1830.

Chapter IV

I took my leave of his lordship, and went home with a heavy heart, not knowing how my wife would take the matter. I informed her of the whole affair. She was more readily reconciled to it than I expected, being always of a most easy and contented disposition. From the account of our good friend Mr. Lindesay and what I had read of America, our conversation being turned to that interesting country, we made up our minds to visit the New World. I, therefore, busied myself in making out my accounts according to order, which gave me no uneasiness. When we had got all things settled in London, we took leave of our good friends, and with our two children took a journey to my native place, the city of Worcester, to bid farewell to my venerable father, my brothers and friends. At Worcester I became acquainted with a clergyman, in a singular kind of way; we met merely by chance. It is wonderful how, where congeniality of disposition exists, how soon and firmly friendship gets cemented. Such was the case with the gentleman, the Rev. Mr. Parker and myself. He had two livings, one at Hoddingly and another at Dorking, he was a great favourite of the late Duke of Norfolk. We became the most confidential friends. He would often hope my wife and I would alter our minds and remain in England, and that he would contribute half his fortune if we would do so; but our minds were fixed. We remained six months in Worcester. I went to Bristol and engaged our passage to New York. Alas! the time was now come for my father and me to part, never to see each other more in this world. This was a severe trial, it seemed to penetrate the inmost recesses of my heart; but my friend was near me to give me consolation in my present affliction; he was a good and most sincere friend. He proposed to walk with us twelve miles, on the road; he informed me by the way that he should soon get married to a lady after his own disposition — a most amiable one I am certain.

We now arrived at our destination, where we dined together for the last time; when the moment of separation arrived, we embraced and separated in hope of corresponding after my arrival in America; but alas, fate had decided it otherwise. This good and worthy man was inhumanly murdered by a villain who shot him by the persuasion and bribery of the justice of peace who lived in the parish of Hoddingly, where Mr. Parker was rector. The body of this villain has lately been found, and it has come out that he himself was murdered by the justice and his abettors. This justice, the greatest villain of the two, by dying a twelve-month before the discovery, escaped justice in this world. I have dwelt long enough on this unhappy subject, and now proceed to give the reader an account of the misfortunes and occurrences that attended me throughout the period of forty years and upwards.

The Rev. George Parker, Rector of Oddingley near Droitwich, was murdered eleven years after he and Benjamin Sanders became friends. Turbeville described the murders at Oddingley near Droitwich, in 1806, as follows: – "The annals of crime record few tragedies so fearful in their reactment, so mysterious in their present concealment, so singular in their ultimate discovery as the Oddingley murders. A clergyman is shot at noonday, while walking in his own fields – the assassin and the motive are perfectly known, yet he eludes justice, and suddenly and for ever disappears. At last, when twenty-four years have elapsed, the body of the murderer is strangely discovered."

The clergyman was murdered because of a bitter dispute between himself and local farmers and landowners about the payment of part of their crops as tithes. Parsons had been receiving tithes since Saxon times, when a tenth of the agricultural produce of a parish had to be given. The Rev. George Parker, as a Rector, was entitled to receive the greater tithe on corn, grain and hops. The payment of tithes was a continual source of dispute between parsons and farmers until the Tithe Commutation Act of 1836, by which Act the payment of tithes in kind was commuted to a payment in money.

The real villain behind the murder of the Rev. George Parker appears to have been the local landowner and magistrate Captain Evans, who had conspired with Mr. Banks, a farm bailiff of Hanbury, Mr. J. Barnett, a farmer, Mr. Taylor, a farrier, Thomas Clewes, a farmer and with Richard Hemming, a Droitwich carpenter, to murder the parson.

On the morning of midsummer day, 1806, Bromsgrove fair day, the parson was walking in his fields when he was shot in the side from behind a hedge. He shouted, "Murder", and the assassin ran forward and hit him on the head with the gun butt until he was dead. The shouts and shots brought people to the scene, but they were threatened off with the gun. They recognised the murderer as Richard Hemming, the carpenter. A woman saw him emerge from a wood and go to the house of Captain Evans, but from there no trace of him was found until twenty-four years later. In 1830, the skeleton of Richard Hemming was found, when a barn which had belonged to Thomas Clewes was being taken down. Thomas Clewes was arrested upon suspicion of Hemming's murder, and he then alleged that Captain Evans and the other men had killed Hemming twenty-four years before, on the day after the parson was shot. Clewes, Banks and Barnett were charged with aiding and abetting the murder of Hemming, but all three were found not guilty. Captain Evans, the ringleader, and Taylor both escaped justice by dying before 1830. The strength of feeling against paying tithes to parsons can be judged by the reaction of Oddingley to the news of the acquittal of the three men. Ignoring the anger of the Rector, the church bells were rung and the men who had been involved in the murder of the parson and of Hemming went scot free.

Chapter V

In which the Sanders family almost perish during their storm-tossed crossing of the Atlantic Ocean to America, and are almost captured by pirates.

This picture of white slaves in Algiers shows what the fate of the Sanders family would have been if their ship had been captured by the Algerian pirates in 1792. Some of the fetters weighed 25 lbs.

Chapter V.

Oceanic voyages in wooden sailing ships were dangerous enterprises when Benjamin Sanders, his wife and two young children sailed to America in 1792. Distances still varied according to the wind and weather, and a favourable wind and a spell of fine weather might make all the difference between a voyage taking weeks or months. The ship carrying Benjamin Sanders and his family from Bristol to New York ran into two terrible storms and the voyage lasted six weeks and three days. One of these storms lasted five nights and five days, during which time, they were confined in a dark wooden box or cabin below decks. The battering received by the ship during this storm was so great that no food could be prepared or even obtained, and Benjamin Sanders thought that his family would die from starvation.

News travelled very slowly between the continents at the mercy of the wind and weather until very recently. In the year following the Sanders's voyage to America, westerly gales kept the news of the execution of the French King Louis XVI and Queen Marie Antoinette from crossing the Atlantic Ocean for weeks. They were executed in January 1793 but the news of the murder did not reach America until April 1793. As F. Braudel has pointed out, "News was a luxury commodity, worth more than its weight in gold."

The danger of being attacked by pirates or by privateers was also a very real one. No sooner than the Sanders's ship had survived one storm, than it was being hunted by a pirate ship from Algiers, on the coast of Barbary. Four people on the ship had been captured recently by pirates from Algiers and had been released by the intervention of the American government. Pirate ships from Algiers had preyed on ships for centuries. Algiers had a large population, about one third of whom were slaves, employed as craftsmen, labourers or as oarsmen in the galleys. There were said to be about eight hundred European slaves in Algiers in 1788. The ransoming of the more important or wealthy captives was an important business in the port. If the pirates had succeeded in capturing the English ship, and if the Sanders family had been captured alive, they would certainly have been enslaved in Algiers until they were ransomed, and a woman captive was considered the property of the crew until the ship returned to Algiers. It was therefore not surprising that young Mrs. Sanders was more afraid of her fate at the hands of the pirates than of drowning in the storm. During the Napoleonic Wars (1793 – 1815) the pirates of Algiers flourished, and became such a menace to merchant ships that the British Navy bombarded the pirate nest at Algiers in 1816, and destroyed its main industry of robbery with violence on the high seas.

When arived at Bristol, we were detained by a misfortune happening to the ship; part of her cargo was obliged to be reshipped which occasioned some detention, and caused us some uneasiness; but at last we sailed with a cheerful breeze and good company. We had two French gentlemen, an American Captain and his nephew who had been just released from the barbarity of the Algerines, by the American Government, and other passengers, which made altogether a very amusing and agreeable company. We now lost sight of our native land, and launched into the wide Atlantic Ocean. Now came on sea-sickness and misery in the extreme, which lasted about three days. This was a wonderful change in life to me and my wife, but she bore it better than I did, being a very kind, easy disposition; as to myself, I was more irritable, but soon reconciled by a little reason on such occasions. My wife and children now became my special care, which was much required, for there came on a most tremendous gale of wind; orders were given from the Captain to lash all things tight above and below, and to make up the dead lights in the cabin. Of all things this appeared to us the most horrible command, being shut out from the light of heaven; my wife and two children (Benjamin and Amelia), the latter two years and a half old, and the former one year and a half. I admired my wife's fortitude in this awful situation; the wind increasing, blew in the most dreadful storm the Captain said he ever saw; now the helm was lashed, and the ship left to the mercy of the waves, which arose mountains high. The storm still increasing, the tremendous noise occasioned by the dreadful waters, and the wind's violent passage through the bare poles of the ship, was horrible in the extreme. Below all was silent, everyone seemingly waiting and expecting the great ocean to overwhelm us and put a period to our existence in this world. Three days and three dismal nights passed away in this manner. I often went on deck, but I was obliged to be lashed to something, otherwise I should have been swept to eternity in a moment. Here I could contemplate the vast Atlantic Ocean, clothed in the Almighty's awful garment, a sight which it is out of the power of the imagination of man to conceive, or his tongue to express.

The wind now began to abate, but the sea became more and more agitated, lifting the ship an amazing height, and descending to an unimaginable depth. This was more horrible than the storm itself; now I was confined below; the vast waves of the sea breaking over the ship, rendering it impossible for me to go on deck. We were tossing in this dreadful manner for two most dismal days and nights more; the sailors were very good in rendering every assistance to us, but, poor fellows, they could not assist themselves; they found it impossible to get at any provisions either for themselves or the passengers. We mercifully outlived this most awful affliction; had it lasted a day and night longer, I believe my wife and myself must have expired in each other's arms, being worn out with suffering and want of nourishment, for what little provision we could get we gave to our dear children. I never saw my wife so amiable as she appeared at this period. When I went to her berth she was giving to her children their last morsel, as it seemed, in this world. My feelings were beyond imagination. We laid down resigning ourselves to the Almighty's will. This night, however, a blessed rain descended, and by morning the raging of the sea subsided to a perfect calm.

I was always an early riser on Board a ship. In the morning I got on deck, though in a very weak state, where to my astonishment I beheld the sea as smooth as a looking-glass; the glorious sun was beginning to rise. This sudden change in the nature astonished me, I felt the congenial warmth and comfort, and it served to urge my soul to go forth and enjoy the world. I never forget to address myself night and morning to the grand Creator of all things, and I did so particularly at this time, where I had so much of the majesty of his glory before me. The ship remained in a dead calm for three days and nights, which gave us time to recruit our strength. The wind now blew fair, and we were all cheerful, going at the rate of near eight knots an hour. The children were very good, and diverted all on board in fine weather. We passed on in this very agreeable manner for upwards of a week. The late storm had driven us a long way to the southward, which lengthened our voyage very much. We were going in a cheerful manner, when the sailor at the helm cried, "A sail." The two Captains ran up on deck, and with their glasses could just see the vessel and that a gun was fired to bring us to. After spying a good while, Captain Ricon cried, "Oh my God, its an Algerine cruiser!" She was making up very fast, and another gun was fired. Our Captain put his ship on her favourite tack and crowded all the sail he could. Another gun with ball whistled and dropped very near us. Poor Captain Ricon and his nephew were in a dreadful state of alarm, though not more so than all on board. We armed ourselves, I having a gun, which I charged, and others with handspikes or any weapon of defence; we were all prepared to fight. We could perceive the enemy come up, notwithstanding all our Captain's exertions; this was a most alarming crisis. The boatswain was at the helm; he had not been there long before he cried out, "Hurrah! hurrah! its all gone." We could see that the Algerines masts were all gone overboard, to the unspeakable joy of us all. My wife felt more uneasiness on this occasion than she did in the late great storm. We congratulated each other on this wonderful escape from those barbarians, and gave the sailors a good share of what makes them cheerful. They put the ship about. The wind being fair, she continued her course towards the New World, passing over the banks of Newfoundland with a fine breeze, but foggy weather.

Soon after we got over the Banks, came on a tremendous storm lasting two days and two nights. We had now got a little inured to a seafaring life, but this storm was really dreadful, though not of so long duration as the great storm, as we always called it. The great storm lasted five days and five nights; this, thank the Almighty, was of only two days and nights' duration, then rain, and a dead calm afterwards; this was about a day and a night's duration, making about five days' detention on our voyage. Now the wind became fair, and a cheering glass was given to the sailors, for they were deserving good fellows. We had fine weather until we came in sight of Long Island; with all our storms and detention we made our passage in six weeks and three days.

The coat of arms used by Benjamin Sanders was distinctive and amusing with three elephants' heads erased per chevron, sable and argent on the shield. The crest consisted of another elephant's head erased sable on a wreath of the colours. The Sanders or Saunders family of Buckinghamshire and Northamptonshire used this coat of arms at least as early as Elizabethan times. The Sanders coat of arms has recently been uncovered decorating one of the Elizabethan panels in a house called Canons Ashby in Northamptonshire. Canons Ashby has belonged to the Dryden family since the 16th century and now belongs to the National Trust.

Chapter VI

In which Benjamin makes buttons in New York and almost dies from yellow fever, saving himself by his own remedy.

New York in 1757. In the centre is Trinity Church and on the left wharves and a fort.

New York in 1798 as Benjamin Sanders knew it. The picture is divided into two sections which should be joined together to give one long view. The artist's position was on Brooklyn Heights. The artist was M. Julien de St. Memin.

Chapter VI.

When the Sanders family arrived safely in New York, in 1792, the successful American rebellion against British rule had ended less than ten years before. Many people in Britain still spoke of the Americans as rebels. When George Washington, the new republic's first President, died in 1799, Robert Southey reported, "It was not thought fitting (in Britain) that any respect should be paid to the memory of a man whom the Sovereign considered as a rebel and a traitor." New York in the 1790's had a population of about thirty-thousand, and was smaller than Bromsgrove is now. Haarlem and Yonkers had not yet become suburbs of New York and were still farming areas where one of Benjamin Sanders's wealthy friends, Mr. De Lancey owned estates.

Benjamin Sanders found a great demand for his abilities as a button-maker and fashionable tailor in New York, and soon built up a prosperous business. It appears that he immediately set to work making cloth-covered buttons at his address in Cherry Street. He found a way of making buttons neatly in the shape of a sugar loaf, which were the latest fashion in England, and which were in short supply in New York, where people wanted to copy English fashions. He also established a thriving tailoring business for wealthy people in New York, obtaining many orders from people known to George Clinton, the Governor of New York. By 1794, he had also established a prosperous tannery in Lamingburg, one hundred and twenty miles north of New York, importing raw deer skins from New Orleans.

Although good fortune smiled on his business ventures, Benjamin Sanders was afflicted with poor health while in New York. Many Europeans found their health deteriorating for the first few months in the new North American environment, particularly in New York, whose summers are hotter than those in Jamaica. Unfortunately for the Sanders family, an epidemic of yellow fever spread from the West Indies to North America in 1794. This epidemic had begun on the island of Grenada and it was alleged that "this malignant pestilential fever" had been brought in a ship from West Africa to Grenada. The Atlantic slave trade was still flourishing in the 1790's, with ship loads of slaves from West Africa arriving in the West Indies and in America. The yellow fever spread rapidly in the West Indies in 1793, killing thousands of people, and the dreaded disease reached Philadelphia and New York in 1794.

Two members of the Rose family, living next door to the Sanders family in Cherry Street, New York died from yellow fever at this time. By a strange coincidence William Rose and his family were from Bromsgrove. William Rose had been a grocer in Bromsgrove and had recently emigrated to America. They belonged to the Rose family who were sextons and parish clerks of St. John's Church for five generations. According to Benjamin Sanders, William Rose was one of the first people in New York to develop yellow fever, after visiting ships from the West Indies, in order to buy articles cheaply from French emigrants who had fled from the French Revolution. The Roses, father and son, and Benjamin Sanders went down with yellow fever during July, the hottest month of the year in New York. Scenes recalling the plague in medieval Europe took place in New York. People were too frightened to visit or take care of friends and relatives stricken with the illness, with the tell-tale black vomit and yellow skin. Even negro slaves belonging to Mr. De Lancey refused to tend Benjamin Sanders.

In the following year of 1795, yellow fever again raged in New York during the summer, but Benjamin Sanders had wisely taken his family to Lamingburg to avoid the heat of New York. Thousands of people fled from the city during that summer as the fever claimed many victims, and the city became almost deserted. Even in Lamingburg the very hot summer brought widespread dysentry, arousing the fears of the Sanders family.

Sailing by Long Island was a most delightful sight at this time, the peach trees in blossom, we were much gratified. Being near land, our usual appetites returned, and we began to relish our food which had not been the case during the whole of the voyage. The next day was Sunday; in the morning we saw Sandy Hook on Staten Island. A signal for a pilot to come on board was answered with quickness that was astonishing, up to us came a sloop, one of the cleanest, most beautiful vessels I ever saw. The pilot came on board and took charge of the ship, and conducted her through the Narrows into the fine spacious harbour of New York. A finer day never shone, everything looked to great advantage to us, after being so long at sea. Sailing past the Battery, a great promenade for ladies and gentlemen, I never saw so many clean well dressed people in my life. About four o'clock in the afternoon the ship came to anchor, when with cordial congratulations we parted with our fellow voyagers and never saw each other more.

We went to live in Cherry Street, in order to prepare for business, which soon answered my expectation. At this time in England, buttons in the form of a sugar loaf were worn, and the Americans are always fond of the English fashions; all the buttons of this description were used, and none to be got. Necessity set my head and hands to work, and with a vast deal of trouble I made some queer things. This was theory, but at last practice made perfect, and I accomplished my design. I made them with cloth in a particular manner, according to my own invention; by practice I at last made buttons exceedingly neat, which was the occasion of my getting a very good business, and I was very much pleased with it.

I carried on a correspondence with my old draper's son (Wm. F.) who had gone into business for himself. We agreed to carry on a mercantile intercourse. I got him to send me out a foreman, who arrived safe, and proved a very good servant. I also got acquainted with a merchant from New Orleans, from whom I purchased raw deer-skins, and remitted to Wm. F. This promised to turn out a very good thing, but it turned out otherwise, for as soon as he could see an opportunity, he took the advantage, and turned out to be a chip off the old block, his father. This correspondence I, therefore, closed. My neighbours were very agreeable and sociable; among the rest was a Mrs. De Lancey, who was very partial to my wife and children, and who became a most welcome companion to my wife. She had a son by her first husband; his name was Morgan, a most accomplished and complete gentleman in his manners. Mrs. De Lancey's present husband was left guardian to this young man, who was bred to the Law, and became so well beloved by Mr. De Lancey, that he could not have been more so had he been his own son. Mr. De Lancey was a gentleman of vast landed property, and a member of Congress, a person of sound principles and agreeable manners. My neighbours on the other side were English, a Mr. Rose of Bromsgrove, with a very agreeable family, particularly the eldest son, who was about my own age. We became in a very short time inseparable companions.

One morning Mrs. De Lancey was with me and my wife, when Mr. Rose came in; there was not, to me, one agreeable quality in this man, he was of coarse principles, in politics violent and obstinate. He came to me saying, "Well, Mr.

*Sanders, I have bought a bargain, of a poor French emigrant, of those jewels,"
showing them to me at the same time, and adding that he had bought them for
one quarter of their value. Mrs. De Lancey being present, looked at him with
indignation, and rose saying, "For shame, Sir, to be such a wretch as to take such
advantages of the unfortunate," and went away immediately. This severe rebuke
met with our complete concurrence. Mr. Rose, was I found, in the habit of going
in a boat in order to get on board vessels from the West Indies. To buy bargains
was his delight, but his mode of proceeding was the occasion of my almost losing
my life. He came home from one of these profitable excursions one evening very ill.
My companion, his son William, came to tell me the doctors had been with his
father, and said his disease was the yellow fever, got by his habit of going on board
vessels from the West Indies. He was a corpse in three days. From the
commencement of this malignant disorder the family's situation was truly
mournful, the fever began to spread itself to all parts of the town. My companion
was taken in the same way as his father. This occasioned unspeakable uneasiness
to my wife and self, and I sat up and attended to him. One night there was no
pacifying him if I was not present; the anxiety between two such friends on this
dreadful occasion can well be imagined. In the morning I went home wearied and
with sunken spirits; my wife persuaded me to lie down and get some little repose.
When I rose I found myself a little refreshed; this was about 3. o'clock in the day. I
went to my companion; his mother was feeding him with some soup. He was
complaining the soup was not good, and Mrs. Rose, very imprudently took up
part of what was left in the basin, and put into my mouth, saying, "Is not this
very good soup, Mr. Sanders?" My attention was drawn too much to my
companion that I did not take heed, and I swallowed the contents, which I had no
sooner done than I was immediately seized with malignant disease, for my blood
seemed to curdle and I felt my whole frame affected. I saw my friend was in a
dying state; in a load of grief I took my last farewell of him. I went home and
acquainted my wife with my unhappy situation. Her apprehensions were no less
than my own, and she became much alarmed, reflecting bitterly on Mrs. Rose's
conduct.*

*I found the next day I was seized with this dreadful disorder, and I was
delirious the whole of the night. In the morning my wife got three of the most
skilful doctors to attend me, but in some way which I cannot account for, I took a
dislike to them, and would not take their medicine, but desired my wife not to give
it to me. I made sure I should be a corpse in less than two days. I had a friend who*

took upon himself to manage my affairs for the benefit of my wife and children. On the night I expected to be my last, being exceedingly ill, before I went to bed I begged of my wife to make a large quantity of camomile tea and give me after I was in bed, and to keep some blankets warm by the fire and put them upon me one by one, until I could bear them no longer. I took my leave of my beloved children and partner, thinking now the bitterness of death was passed; I went to bed, resigning myself to the Almighty's will, being certain before morning to be in another and better world. I lay down in bitter anguish and took, as we both imagined, the last embrace. This was the middle of July, the hottest season of the year in New York. I had the perserverance to lie under the bedclothes until suffocation almost took place; in the course of three hours I burst into the most profuse perspiration that any mortal ever endured. I was not delirious as I was the night before. I now put my head above the bedclothes, and took into my lungs a most refreshing portion of fresh air. It is impossible to describe the relief it gave me. I looked up and saw my wife, who in her watchful anxiety relieved me with a dry shirt. I shifted myself into a dry part of the bed and went to sleep, which I was much in want of; I slept till morning. I was in such a state of weakness that my wife was obliged to dress me like an infant. She got me a chicken for my dinner. The doctors came in at this time, expecting to find I was dead; to their great astonishment I was alive. One took my hand and another the other, and pronounced me a happy man, as my disorder had taken a favourable turn. By the means I took with myself I had weakened the malignity by dispersing its fatal strength through the whole of my constitution. I became as vividly yellow from the crown of my head to the very soles of my feet. Those that die in this malignant disorder are never yellow below the middle of the body. This convinces me, that the means my wife and I took to force a violent perspiration, proved a remedy for the disorder. I remained very weak for some time. The good Mrs. De Lancey could not persuade any one of her black servants to give us the least aid, but came herself and assisted my wife in nursing me. The disorder raged in a most dismal manner, people trembled to see relations or friends. When I got a little strength, I was anxious to get a little fresh air, but people when I was going to the Battery (a favourite promenade) would run away, and avoid me as much as possible; certainly my colour was fearfully yellow.

One day one of my doctors came and asked me if I would inform him how I treated myself in the dreadful yellow fever; I told him that for the sake of mankind, I would inform him of the whole particulars, which I did; his name was Smith, health-doctor for the city. We had a long conversation; he seemed to approve of my reasoning in general. I condemned calomel, or any preparation from mercury, which I well knew was the general prescription of the doctors for this disorder; but they were all so prejudiced in favour of their system, that it was useless to argue with them, though I was convinced by the late practice on myself, that the only remedy is to force a violent perspiration. Two of my doctors were afterwards taken ill and died, Dr. Smith and Dr. Yeoel. I have dwelt longer on this subject in hopes that my experience may be of service to those that my be in a similar situation.

Benjamin Sanders was very wise in rejecting the useless and often dangerous remedies offered by the doctors of his day and in applying his own remedy of sweating out the disease. It either killed within three to seven days, or allowed the victim a rapid recovery followed by life-long immunity to further attacks. The main treatment offered by doctors was copious blood letting and strong doses of preparations of mercury, especially calomel, which was widely recommended by doctors as a purgative. There was a lot of overdosing with mercury and also excessive bleeding well into the nineteenth century for all kinds of diseases. Robert Southey commented very aptly on the use of preparations of mercury, "Every man his own poisoner."

Benjamin Sanders was, however, mistaken in blaming his contraction of yellow fever on drinking soup from a basin which had been used by a yellow fever victim. During the nineteenth century there were bitter quarrels between doctors about the causes of yellow fever and its treatment. It was very puzzling how the disease ran through a town, with relatively short jumps from one victim to the next, but sometimes skipping several houses, and those in daily contact with the victim might escape altogether. Thirty-five years after Benjamin Sanders caught yellow fever, a very courageous Lt. Mackinnial of H.M.S. Sybille demonstrated that yellow fever was not contagious like smallpox, by drinking a glass of black vomit from a yellow fever victim. Later in the nineteenth century it was discovered that yellow fever was transmitted by a particular kind of mosquito, the aedes aegypti. The bites of this mosquito convey a parasite to human beings, which causes the disease.

Machines used in the manufacture of buttons in the eighteenth century.

Chapter VII

In which he helps a poor English farmer and his family, and establishes a leather manufactory in Laminburg, and nearly shoots a Red Indian.

Fashions in America when Benjamin Sanders arrived. Note the large buttons. Benjamin Sanders's friends the De Lanceys lived in similar style. The picture is of the Chief Justice of the Supreme Court Oliver Ellsworth with his wife at Windsor, in Connecticut in 1792. Artist: Ralf Earl.

Chapter VII.

*By the care of my wife and Mrs. De Lancey, I began to recover fast. Mr.
and Mrs. De Lancey, Mr. Morgan and ourselves, lived on the most agreeable
terms. My wife and I were just going to dinner one day, when in came a person
of the name of Cock. He was a farmer much connected with my wife's family
in Somersetshire; he had been in the habit of coming to London often when we
were in business there. I was exceedingly partial to this man; his conversation,
with a little touch of Somerset dialect, was always very agreeable. As he was the
last man we thought to meet in this part of the world, we were very happy to
see him, and he sat down with us to a very welcome dinner. Of course, the
conversation was all on the farmer's affairs, which had been a continuance of
misfortunes, so that reading of America he was determined to try his fortune here;
but misfortune had still followed him, he had been in New York with his wife
and part of his family near three months, all ill during the whole time, and the
poor man himself was changed from a fine handsome person to a languid and
sickly appearance. Such is the case in general with Europeans at first coming into
the American climate. The farmer now related to us what was the state of his
family; he was in extreme want, and in a strange country, his little property all
exhausted. His great trouble at present was his doctor's bill, which he said it was
out of his power to pay. I was anxious to see his wife and children; his wife was
one of those kind women whose greatest pleasure is in assisting their families to
enjoy the blessings and comforts of life. Poor Mrs. Cock was much altered, looking
pale and languid, surrounded with a numerous family of seven children, much
in the same situation as herself. I left as it were, my heart with them and requested
the farmer to take me to his doctor, whom he was in so much anxiety about; the
doctor seemed a very good sort of man, and the farmer spoke well of him. I discharged
the account, which occasioned unspeakable joy to this good couple and their family.*

*Our thoughts were now fixed on this worthy family. Being so intimate with
the De Lancey family, I went to Mr. De Lancey next day, and said to him, "Sir,
you have large landed property, could you not find employment for an English*

farmer?" He said he could find employment for many if he could get them. I was immediately struck with a feeling that a road was here opened for our beloved farmer and his family. I informed Mr. De Lancey of the whole matter I have related above; the good gentleman warmed my very heart by saying I might bring my friend, and he would take him to his farm at Yenkous, which is distant from New York about 16 miles. He said he had an estate called Haerlem, about half the distance, but he should take my farmer to the farthest estate first, and call at Haerlem on their return. I informed Mr. De Lancey I would be any security for Mr. Cock, as I had every confidence in him, having known him so long. I returned to my wife with a heart full of pleasure, and she received the news with a transport of joy. I went to communicate it to my farmer, and directed to come to me next morning, to go with Mr. De Lancey to look over a farm; I received showers of blessings from his amiable family. Next day the farmer came cleanly dressed, and looking very respectable. I introduced him to Mr. De Lancey who took him to his estate in Yenkous, my wife and I waiting with much anxiety for his return. Mr. De Lancey engaged him, to his great satisfaction. This good news seemed to complete our happiness. Mr. Cock and his family removed in a few days to a handsome house, comfortably furnished, having their habitation, firing, and other necessaries, all free of expense. Mr. De Lancey was to stock the farm with all things requisite, to find seed, the farmer to do the labour, and they were to divide the profits.

Mr. Morgan had taken a great liking to the farmer's youngest boy, and kept him in New York; he was about eight years old, and seemed to be blessed with a most agreeable disposition; he, I am confident, was well provided for.

In about three months, Mr. De Lancey went up to his estate, to see how his farmer went on. At his return I was anxious to know what satisfaction my friend had given. To my great pleasure I found he had given more satisfaction than ever could be expected. Mr. Cock had left in England the elder part of his children. Mr. De Lancey had taken so much to the family, that he advised the farmer to send for them; they were fortunate in a very quick passage, and arrived sooner than was expected. There were three sons, fine, strong, well-made young men, and a daughter, one of the finest and handsomest young women I ever saw. They were placed on the Haerlem estate, on the same terms as the father and mother were on that at Yenkous.

All things now smiled around us. I buried myself in a concern which I was establishing at a place called Lamingburg, up from New York about 120 miles, *in order to evade the hot season in New York. This was in the manufacturing of leather from the raw skins; having some little knowledge of that business, and knowing some poor Englishmen of that profession, I engaged them to go to Lamingburg to manufacture. I sent up a large quantity of raw deer-skins from New Orleans, for my men to work up. I found in them very excellent managers, and exceedingly skilful workmen. I soon found I could place such confidence in them that I might leave them. When I returned to New York I found them all happy; the farmer and his family giving more and more satisfaction. Mr. De Lancey grew very attached to them, which gave us and Mr. Morgan great pleasure. Mrs. De Lancey also became exceedingly fond of my wife and children; and Johnny, as she always called her son, grew as fond of the farmer's little boy. We were thus a very agreeable society, and spent as pleasant a time as can be imagined, until the hot season began to approach. With all our family we then took our departure for the north, to my leather manufactory, which I found had been managed in a manner that far exceeded my expectations. In a little time we heard that the dreadful yellow fever was beginning to rage in New York, and causing it to be deserted by its inhabitants. We also found it very hot, which kept us in continual alarm, as people were very sickly with a dysentry.*

I was fond of shooting, and here was plenty of game in the woods of every description, and very large squirrels, the most delicious eating I ever tasted. In coming out of a wood one day, I was near stepping on an Indian and his squaw, with a blanket over them and a tomahawk on his breast. I was much alarmed, as I had not far passed them when I heard a most barbarous shout from the man; I turned round and beheld him sitting up with his weapon in his hand. I ran quickly up to him and presented my gun, telling him I would shoot him dead if he offered to rise; seeing his danger he quietly lay down. I never in my life felt more happy than when the alarm had passed, and I came to calm reflection, on this occasion; for I must have shot the Indian in order to save my own life, and had I done so, I am certain it would have embittered the remainder of my days. I thanked the Almighty for this deliverance. I was now in the noise of a wonderful fall of water, called the Cohoes; it is the close of a large river called the Mohawk and falls down a precipice of tremendous depth. The roaring of these waters are heard at the distance of many miles; I went to the top, which is like ascending to another world. This grand scene must amaze every beholder.

Chapter VIII

In which he meets an extraordinary slave, and retrieves a pair of pantaloons from another swindler, bringing a change of heart in a young man.

Seal of the Committee for the Abolition of the Slave Trade formed in 1787.

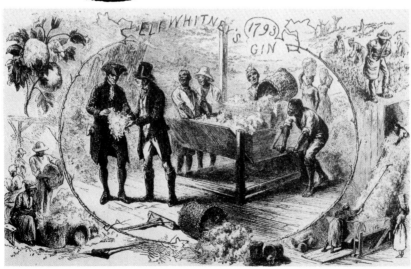

The invention of the cotton-gin revitalized America's cotton industry, which was built on a constant supply of slave-labour from West Africa.

Chapter VIII

Most wealthy people in America had negro slaves in the 1790's, like
Benjamin Sanders's friends the De Lanceys. Benjamin Sanders appears
to have accepted slaves, as most people still did then, as part of the
natural order. It was another seventy years before the American Civil
War broke out in which Americans fought each other over the issue of
slavery. The only astonishment which Benjamin Sanders expressed about
a slave in America was his encounter with an albino negro slave. Albino
negroes were called white Moors (Africans) by early European travellers
in Africa, who marvelled when they found such negroes with snowy
white skin, snow white hair and pink eyes. They were often believed to
have magical powers in Africa. General Cornwallis, the commander of
the English army who surrendered to the Americans at Yorktown in
1781, tried unsuccessfully to buy this remarkable albino slave from his
master. By the 1780's opposition to the slave trade and to slavery began
to appear in America and in Britain and was usually led by Quakers. The
Society for the Abolition of the Slave Trade was founded in Britain in
1787, and nine of the twelve members were Quakers. Benjamin Sanders's
silence on this issue suggests that he was one of the majority who did not
support the abolitionist cause in the 1790's.

*After admiring this wonderful work of providence, I walked on towards a
slave, as I thought; he was digging on the other side of a fence from me. I said to
him, "My friend, who lives at that farm house?" I expected to be answered by a
black man, when up stood the most frightful being eyes ever beheld. I was in great
doubt whether to run, or what to do. This was a white black man. He answered
that it was his master's house. I soon found he was perfectly harmless. I went to
him over the fence; his head and face were preposterously large; he had large pink
coloured eyes, a prodigious large flat nose, with large expanded nostrils, and
monstrous projecting lips; his skin was of the most delicate white. I soon found that
he was a good natured and communicative man. He said he was glad I did not*

*run away as many people had done. "Den, (he said) he haloo, and often had fun."
This extraordinary being suffered me to examine him minutely; he held down his
head; the texture of his hair was more delicate than it is possible to describe. I began
to be delighted with his company, and examined his skin, which was in accordance
with his head and face. I found no ignorance in this man, for he gave very
satisfactory answers to my enquiries. He had good principles of love and gratitude
towards his master. He told me Lord Cornwallis saw him, and went to his master
and offered a vast deal of money for him. His master told Lord Cornwallis that if
he could persuade the man to go with him, he would take the offer, otherwise no
money would purchase him. Lord Cornwallis talked to him and said if he would
go with him he would make a great man of him. He told his Lordship he had "a
very good massa, and dat he should soon die if he was taken away from his good
massa." I asked him if there were any more white people in his family, he said,
"No". He had a wife and three children all blacks, and slaves to his master; he
said there was one white man born in his family every so many moons, but there
was only himself now. The showing of this man in England would, I am certain,
produce a wonderful deal of money.*

*I had ten miles to go home to Lamingburg, thinking of my new
acquaintance. A few days afterwards I took my wife to the Cohoes, which she was
more amazed at even than myself. Afterwards we went to the farmer's to see my
white black man, who struck my wife with more astonishment I believe, than he
did me. We found all the family at home; we drank tea with the master and his
wife, whom we found to be very kind people, and that all was true that the white
black slave had told me. He had his wife and three of the most handsome black
children we ever saw; the contrast between the father, wife and children, was
astonishing. We were very agreeably entertained, and returned to Lamingburg,
where all my business was going on exceedingly well, and turned out to be very
good profit, very satisfactory for the first year's establishment.*

*My principal employment was shooting; coming home one day, a dove flew
across, which I shot, the most innocent bird, and decked out in the most splendid
plumage that can be imagined. I picked it up, and it died in my hand. I had bitter
reflections on this transaction, and made a sacred promise to myself, that I would
never more be an enemy to the lovely feathered tribe. I came home, put up my
gun, and never became a sportsman again.*

*The weather being very hot, and all of us were sickly and languid, praying
for the cooler season to commence. At length we were informed that the yellow*

fever was gone, and New York had become healthy, we therefore took our departure for New York, where we found everything to our wishes, my farmer (as I called him) going on exceedingly well, and Mr. De Lancey gave me such a description of the whole of this lovely family, as often gave me inexpressible pleasure in times of affliction. My readers can well judge of the pleasure and happiness that reigned among us. New York became gay, and sorrow disappeared. A singular circumstance, however, occurred, which occasioned me some uneasiness. General Clinton gave a ball to most of the gentry, and I was busy for the occasion. A young gentleman came, having, as he represented, just arrived from the West Indies; he said he was a nephew of Mr. Sandys of Long Island. I knew this gentleman to be a wealthy man. The nephew stated that he was invited to the ball of General Clinton, and wanted a very handsome suit of clothes to wear on the occasion. I engaged to make them. He then asked if, in the first place, I would have the goodness to furnish him a pair of pantaloons by the morrow, which request I punctually attended to. At the time appointed his pantaloons were ready, and his ball suit in sufficient forwardness. He begged leave to retire into a room, for the convenience of putting on the new pantaloons. When he returned he asked if I would get the old ones repaired, observing they would do to wear on board a ship, as he was soon to return to the West Indies. I asked him if it was convenient for him to call and just put on his coat before it was quite finished, or if he pleased I would wait on him; he said, "By no means", he should be going by about three next day, and he would call in at that time. I lived opposite to a Colonel Willett, who was a very agreeable neighbour; he came over to me, saying, "Mr. Sanders, I observed young Sandys to go into your house;" I answered in the affirmative. "Well, (said the Colonel) I came as a neighbour, and a friend to put you on your guard; I assure you he is one of the greatest profligates in New York," adding that he was a nephew of Mr. Sandys of Long Island, rope and sailmaker, and one of the best and worthiest gentlemen in the country. "This young man (said he) is his heir, the only being Mr. Sandys adores; but the youth has been corrupted by bad company, and has almost broke his Uncle's heart." The Colonel said a great deal on the amiable disposition of Mr. Sandys, so that I thought him a gentleman very much to be pitied. The Colonel left me, telling me further that there were three writs out against this hopeful boy.

This information worked upon me exceedingly, I scarcely knew how to conduct myself on this occasion, but I finally determined, and acted accordingly. I had a friend whose only son was a little tainted through the influence of bad company; he persuaded me to take this son under my care a little while. I did so, and our kindness soon made an improvement in him; but I was resolved he should be present to see what I had made up my mind to do towards young Sandys. This young gentleman came at the time appointed. I begged my wife's absence, and desired him to walk into the parlour. I took his old pantaloons in my hand, and said to my friend's son, "William, come along with me." Poor William seemed to be a little disturbed, but when all got into the parlour, I locked the door and put the key into my pocket, William staring in great alarm. I turned to young Sandys, saying, "Sir, here are your old pantaloons for you to put on when you have taken off the new ones;" which offer he rejected. I looked sternly at him, and insisted upon it that he should do so before I went out of the room. William now began to cry, seeing my determination. After a vast deal to do, however, my customer took off the new and put on the old pantaloons. This business being settled, I talked to him in as pathetic terms as I was capable of. William now cried and roared most immoderately. After I had commented on his base designs upon me, and how he had obtained the displeasure of his uncle, he burst into a flood of tears, and begged to go. I began to have compassion on him, and told him it would be seen I was not so hard hearted as he might suppose. I then went to my desk and took out fifteen Spanish dollars, telling him there were three writs out against him, and to make the best of his way. He refused my money, and begged to go. I gave him all the good advice I could, pressing the fifteen dollars on him, but he positively refused them. He took his departure respectfully, with such dejection in his countenance as alarmed me, and I repented of what I had done. This was a lesson to poor William, who turned out a most excellent young man, to the happiness of his father and friends. Colonel Willett commended the manner in which I had managed this business, and all parties felt much satisfied; but the recollection worked otherwise with me, and caused me many disagreeable thoughts.

My wife had a sister who was settled at Copenhagen, the capital of Denmark. The last summer being so exceedingly unhealthy, I had been very ill up at Lamingburg; I was declining much in my constitution, to the great alarm of my wife and our beloved friends. Our good old Dr. Young pronounced that my case would terminate fatally if I remained in America much longer, and that the north of Europe would be more proper for me. Our Copenhagen correspondent now worked upon me and my wife, and we made up our minds to make the best of our way to that city. This was a terrible blow to all parties, being so universally united in friendship.

On the approach of our time of departure, one afternoon we were just going to tea, when in came a most respectable gentleman, and requested to be introduced to good Mr. Sanders; when I answered I was that person, he said his name was Sandys, of Long Island, and he came to shower blessings on me and mine that he had at home a reclaimed nephew, returned to him from the West Indies, and that I was the person who had reclaimed him. This was very agreeable news indeed for us. My wife invited him to drink tea with us, and it is impossible there could be three more happy people. He entertained us with all the contents of his nephew's letters, where I was spoken of with the greatest respect, and he had described the exact scene between me, himself and William. We were much delighted in the company of this gentleman; at last, however, he took his leave of us, with his blessing, and we never saw him afterwards. This interview operated very pleasantly on me, as I often found within myself feelings of regret and repentance for the manner in which I had conducted myself towards young Mr. Sandys. The reader's own reflections will save me further description on this agreeable occasion.

I went to Lamingburg, and disposed of my business, and settled William and my foreman in business in Albany, with a genteel stock, good advice, and good prospects; my other servants were more disposed to go further up the country. I took leave of them all and returned to New York, where I engaged the cabin of a neutral ship to Hamburg. Having got my property on board, and the time of our departure drawing near, the thoughts of our separation from so happy a connection can be easier felt than it is in my power to describe. We left the farmer and his family under the friendly care of Mr. and Mrs. De Lancey and Mr. Morgan; better people could not be. The ship was now ready and a general farewell took place, with blessings indescribable. The ship got under way, and we took the last look of our friends, never to see each other more. We were now launched once more on the bosom of the vast Atlantic Ocean. Having now the interesting children, we had a very pleasant and prosperous voyage.

Chapter IX

In which the Sanders family embark once more on the high seas and encounter friendly and hostile French ships and survive another great storm.

Chapter IX.

Benjamin Sanders and his family sailed from America back to Europe in 1795 to begin a new life in Copenhagen. Napoleon was rising to power in France by using cannon to fire on violent mobs in Paris, and there was warfare on the high seas between Britain and revolutionary France, adding to the usual hazards of ocean travel. Britain and France had been at war for two years, and even neutral ships were in danger of being intercepted and plundered by the ships of both nations. Benjamin Sanders chose to sail on a neutral Swedish ship as the safest way of crossing the Atlantic. He objected strongly to Britain's right to search policy, which often resulted in the boarding of neutral ships and the seizure of their cargoes of iron, timber and grain. These goods were seized on the grounds that they were destined for France or for her allies. The British claim to the right of searching neutral ships had caused wars with Holland in the past, and was to cause wars in the future.

The neutral ship carrying the Sanders family was intercepted and boarded by a French man-of-war, but the French commander fortunately, treated Benjamin Sanders in a very civilised manner. A few days later they were in far more danger, when they were fired at by a French ship, and they were saved from being plundered only by the rough weather.

About five miles from the English channel the Captain came very early one morning saying, "Mr. Sanders, get up, we shall have some of your countrymen to see you". We got up and went on deck. There were three men-of-war at a distance in front of us with English colours flying; presently a gun was fired, the colours taken down, and French hoist in their stead. I observed some emotion in our Captain while he was looking through his spy-glass; he turned to me and said, "Oh! Mr. Sanders, they are French, which makes me very unhappy for your sake". I began to remonstrate with him, and hoped he had not deceived me in regard to his papers. By this time came along side our ship a boat full of men, with an officer in a French naval uniform, he was accommodated with a ladder over the side, and coming on deck addressed himself to me; he spoke English perfectly well. At this time, the reader will observe, there was a decree from the French government to destroy every ship and cargo belonging to the English nation. Our Government behaved basely, in the opinion of most men, in suffering the mercantile trade to be destroyed in the ruinous manner it was at that time. The French officer thought I was the Captain; I set him right, and introduced the real Captain, Bandandike, a Swede, who asked my permission to take the French officer down to examine his papers. When this was done the French gentleman came on deck and took my hand in a very polite manner, saying, that though the two nations were at War, it was not the case of individuals. We had half an hour's conversation, which was exceedingly agreeable to all parties.

When the time came for his departure to report to his Commodore we pressed him to take breakfast with us; he admired our children, and said he should return again before we had permission to continue our course. In about an hour, two boats full of men rowing towards us a little alarmed us. The same gentleman came on board with his compliments to us, and a present of two bags of bread, hot from the oven, thinking they might be acceptable to my wife and children; he brought also a large pitcher of wine, but at the same time said, being an Englishman, he was obliged to encumber me with the crew of a ship they had burnt, with its valuable cargo, the Sunday previous. I very readily complied with the Commodore's request, and the unfortunate ship's company came on board, with the Captain and mate. Our Commander expressed an unwillingness to receive them, observing that Sweden was a neutral nation. I told him that I would be answerable for all expenses that might accrue. The French officer and I had again a good deal of conversation; he complained much of the insubordination on board of French ships. I complained of the folly of two such enlightened nations as England and France, in destroying each other's property by the rough hand of war; he perfectly agreed in my opinion. On a signal from the Commodore's ship for him to go, he said he should again return. In a short time he came back with a sufficiency of provisions for the unfortunate ship's company to last them home. The French officer said we might now proceed on our voyage, and we parted in a respectful manner; he was a sensible and polite man. When he got on board, a broadside from the three French ships denoted our departure, which the captain of the unfortunate ship said was a very great mark of respect; he spoke very highly of the French officers. The Commodore gave him, the mate and crew a very handsome sufficiency of money to defray their expenses to London. The Commander of the unfortunate ship whose name was Henderson, said the French Commodore behaved to him with the kindness of a brother.

We now proceeded on our voyage. In about two days the wind blew exceedingly hard, and we were brought to by a single French ship, which kept firing at us the whole day, the weather being so rough they could not board us; if they had, no doubt we should have been plundered without mercy. The kindness of Providence seemed to protect us in times of danger, the winds and waves proved our best friends in this instance. We experienced no more trouble on the voyage. The ship completed the passage from New York to Hamburg in six weeks and three days, which, considering our detention and stoppage in shipping Captain Henderson and fourteen of his crew, was considered a quick passage.

At Hamburg we found a gentleman ready to take charge of and conduct us through the country, with the protection of the German language; this was well contrived by my wife's relations. Our director was a great acquisition; he got everything done for us that necessity required, and proved a most agreeable fellow traveller; a broker being in charge of my property, we took our departure for Copenhagen, and found it a most troublesome journey.

Leaving Hamburg, we passed through Holstein, a very fine country, to Kiel, a Danish town and university. Here we became so fatigued through the miserable mode of travelling, that we found it prudent to rest three days, and then started on another sea voyage. Mr. Lindley, our fellow traveller, engaged a boat to take us over the great belt to Cursue, in Zealand. A very great mistake was made in computing the distance, which proved twice as great as we expected. By the time we had got ten miles out it blew hard, the water very rough, and all of us very sick; the children, however, behaved well. Mr. Lindley did everything in his power to pass pleasantly the times of danger; he sung, and told us many amusing tales, but at last we began to fear we should all be lost. The night approached with terror to us all, but happily the wind kept fair, and with the blessings of the Almighty we fortunately arrived at our destination, but all in a very weak state. We were now on the island of Zealand, and took extra horses in order to get into Copenhagen before the gates of the town were shut. Our expedition from Hamburg excited much astonishment among the Danes. We found our Copenhagen friends very happy to receive us, and remained at my wife's sister's until we got our property from Hamburg, which arrived in very good time.

Chapter X

In which Benjamin the rooter makes suits for the nobility in Copenhagen, establishes a silk manufactory; meets a haughty duchess and the beautiful Madame Bearn.

Top: Nelson raising his telescope to his sightless eye, at the battle of Copenhagen in 1801. Admiral Parker has signalled retreat but Nelson tells Foley, standing behind him, that he cannot see the signal, and the sailor beside him smirks.

Battle of Copenhagen, 1801.

Chapter X.

Mr. Lindley was indefatigable in rendering his services towards us; he provided convenient apartments, where I began business and soon became known, and was recommended to the first noblemen and foreign ambassadors in the kingdom. The Prime Minister and his brothers, all fine well made gentlemen, were very solicitous for my welfare and let no opportunity escape of recommending me; in short I soon became the first tradesman in that metropolis.

There was a gentleman came from Harlangen, with five of the most beautiful little Italian greyhounds I ever saw; they attracted my notice very much. This gentleman's name was Sir Levet Hanson; his secretary (Mr. Roll) was as fond of those interesting animals as Sir Levet himself. I became acquainted with Sir Levet in an odd manner; our sentiments agreeably united, and much friendship subsisted between us. Sir Levet was called away from Copenhagen to Harlangen; at his return I was much pleased when he called at my house one morning, and in conversation remarked that he had been always invited by every English ambassador, to dine with him on the Christmas day, but had not been asked by Sir Benjamin Garlike, who was British ambassador to the court of Denmark at that time. I answered "Sir Levet, you think as I do, that it is of very little consequence; but if you, sir, should have a desire to dine with a Benjamin, come and dine on that day with Benjamin Sanders, where you will be made more welcome, and treated with more respect than you would be by the English ambassador". Sir Levet had a fine pleasant manly countenance, but particularly so on this occasion; he took my hand in a very friendly way, saying, "I most sincerely thank you, Benjamin, but I have an appointment on that day with Sir Brook Boothby, but I will dine with you some day, and we will be very happy." Sir Levet was a most accomplished gentleman; he had lived many years in Italy, and was Chamberlain and Brigadier-General to the Duke of Modena. There was not a man who had more universal knowledge, as I had been told by gentlemen who had seen the world, that he was the most eminent in giving information that they believed existed. This gentleman dined with me on another occasion, and we were all very happy, as he had foretold; subsequently a most affectionate correspondence took place between him and me for many years.

A gentleman arrived at Copenhagen (the Duke of Campocaino) as Neapolitan ambassador. Having the patronage of all the principal nobility at the Court of Denmark, I was ordered to wait on the gentleman, who desired me to make for his servants the most splendid liveries I could invent, and a most elegant court suit for himself, his lady and servants, and he made the most splendid appearance of all the ambassadors who attended the Court of Denmark. On this occasion I exerted all by abilities, which was not considered trifling in their way. The Duke was a very kind, affable gentleman, and expressed himself to me in terms the most satisfactory; even his lady expressed herself much pleased, for the first time since her marriage with the Duke, as her valet expressed himself. She was the most proud, haughty woman I ever saw; the Duke was exactly the reverse, I never was more pleased in waiting on a gentleman in my life. I have often wondered how such contrary tempers could possible exist together.

By the persuasion of her husband, the Duchess begged of me to procure for her the most elegant dresses possible; and out of respect for the Duke I spared no pains to procure such. This passed on till a ship from India arrived, commanded by Captain Blake; there was a very agreeable man, a passenger Dr. Francis, with whom I got very intimate, and he dined with me. One day I asked him if there were any elegant muslin embroidered ladies' dresses on board, as I had seen such from India. I informed him also how I was situated by my promise to the Duke's lady. To my great joy, he told me he had six of the most elegant dresses on board that ever were seen, and that he would smuggle them on shore to oblige me, which he did, I never saw such beautiful articles. I took the Doctor to the Duke's house with them; his excellency seemed much pleased. The doctor waited in the ante-chamber while the Duke and I were admitted into the Duchess's dressing-room. When our choice dresses were shown to this amiable lady, she fell into such a fit of frenzy with the Duke and me, that she threw them at us with such violence of behaviour, that his Excellency made a precipitate retreat, and left me, as I thought, to a severe chastisement; however, in came the doctor, and scrambled all the finery up, swearing all the while about infamous b____, with other contemptuous expressions, and went his way. All I could say or do availed nothing with this fine lady, who led the fashion of Copenhagen. The Duchess, was, in more important particulars, a most unnatural woman, she had two children, and as soon as they were born, she ordered them to be taken away, and never cared what became of them afterwards.

This was the information I received from the servants. I now went to look after the doctor, whom I found at my house. I was going to apologise, but he stopped me by laughing and saying he never saw a better bit of fun in his life. He was so near to her Ladyship's dressing-room that he heard all the goings on there. I was very glad to find my friend, Dr. Francis, so easily pacified.

The ship having to discharge great part of her cargo at Copenhagen, Captain Blake, the doctor and myself got more and more agreeably acquainted. I introduced them to our fellow traveller, Mr. Lindley; he being a young man of very good abilities, gained the esteem of Captain Blake who persuaded him to go to India with him. The ship had to go from Copenhagen to London, and from there to India, Mr. Lindley went with the Captain, and my friend the doctor remained in Copenhagen some time.

I had done a great deal of business for the Duke of Campocaino when I was informed by a gentleman that the Duke had become a ruined man, and that the success of the French in Italy was the cause of it. The Duke sent for me one morning, and informed me that his necessities obliged him to return to Italy, and requested me to make out and deliver my account. Knowing the Duke's unhappy situation I was in a mind to reject his orders by forgiving the debt; if I had possessed words sufficient to avoid hurting the Duke's feelings, I could with great pleasure have done so. When I sent my account according to order, his confidential servant came with the Duke's jewels, and a very polite request to receive them for my security. I returned them, however, by the messenger and desired him to inform the Duke I required no security of any kind. In a few days afterwards a person came and paid my account to the full amount. Shortly after this came a message from the Duke, requesting me to wait on him the next day at eleven o'clock, which I punctually did. When I arrived I found servants, carriages and everything in readiness for travelling. I was conducted into the reception room, when soon came the Duke to me, and took me by the hand and blessed me; I did the same by him, and we took a last farewell, for I never saw this good kind gentleman any more.

I received a letter from Mr. Lindley, not of a very pleasant nature; it appeared that in consequence of a misunderstanding between him and Captain Blake, he had got his property landed and went on shore at the Cape of Good Hope. I had many letters from him, from different parts of the world, surprising and astonishing enough. I also heard from Dr. Francis, who was settled in Wales as a retired gentleman.

Myself, my wife and family began to be pleased with our situation in

Copenhagen, with the very good company and cordial friendship of good Sir Levet Hanson and his secretary. The apartments above those in which we lived were occupied by a Madame Bearn. This lady had been the favourite companion of Gustavus, the late King of Sweden, who was shot by Ankerstrom at a masked ball; she was a Jewess, of a sweet countenance, of a fine shape, and agreeable manners; in short, she was a complete lady. She came to Copenhagen for retirement, having an independent fortune, and was now married to Mr. Bearn, a Jew and a merchant, a most amiable man; he had three children by a former wife and one by his present wife. Our children and Mr. and Mrs. Bearn's being the same in number, and about the same age, became very agreeable playmates, and by their means my wife and I, and Mr. and Mrs. Bearn became intimately acquainted. We were all very happy and going on very well. I had established a silk manufactory, in order to employ some poor silk weavers that came from Spitalfields, but I did not find in them such profitable servants as those I left in America.

I became now in the confidence of all the gentlemen who employed me; they in general treated me more as a companion than as a tradesman. But alas! the news came that the Danes had broken their neutrality, and that an English armament was soon to be expected.

Evening Dress in 1800.

Chapter XI

In which he loses his house and fortune; is parted from his family; is imprisoned and nearly shot during the British bombardment of Copenhagen in 1807.

The British bombardment of Copenhagen in 1807. The spire of Frue Church is in the background. Congreve's flaming rockets can be seen in the sky. Artist: C. A. Lorentzen.

Chapter XI.

Denmark's trade had suffered from the English seizure of cargoes on Danish ships and in 1801 it joined other Baltic powers in a league against England called the "Armed Neutrality of the North". By this time Benjamin Sanders had built up a very prosperous business in Copenhagen, becoming the most fashionable tailor in the Danish capital. The deteriorating relations between England and Denmark flared into open warfare in 1801, when Nelson crippled the Danish fleet at Copenhagen in a battle which he called the most terrible which he had experienced. Fifteen hundred cannon on the English and Danish ships pounded away at each other for four hours before the Danes asked for a truce. Nelson ignored a signal to retreat in this battle by clapping his glass (telescope) to his sightless eye saying, "Now damn me if I do!" It is curious that Benjamin Sanders made no mention of this thunderous battle off Copenhagen, when his country house was so close to the coast, about three-quarters of a mile north of Copenhagen near the Sound. However, Copenhagen escaped from being bombarded by the English fleet in 1801 by accepting the English terms. It was lucky for Benjamin Sanders that an armistice was arranged between Denmark and England in 1801 because an English bombardment would certainly have ruined his business then, as it did six years later.

Benjamin Sanders was able to prosper and live another six years in Denmark after the battle of Copenhagen, until the next English action against the Danes in 1807, which was far more drastic than the limited naval engagement of 1801. Napoleon was at the height of his power in 1807, having defeated the armies of Austria and Prussia and he turned his attention to England. England then stood alone against Napoleon, who had become the master of most of Europe, just as she stood alone against Hitler and Germany's mastery of Europe in 1940. Napoleon began a trade war against England, forbidding France or any of her allies or subject territories to accept English goods. English ships were to be excluded from all European ports in order to strangle England's export trade. Napoleon's plan of bankrupting England needed French control over the whole of Europe, and was called appropriately the Continental System.

England retaliated with a naval blockade of any port which refused to accept English ships. This made it necessary for England to deprive France of ships in order to make the English blockade of European ports effective. Consequently, when the English government heard that Napoleon was planning to seize the Danish navy, it promptly ordered the Danes to hand over their ships to England until the end of the war. Denmark was now caught between two fires: both France and England were threatening to invade that small state. Napoleon told the Danes that they had to choose between a war with France or an alliance with France, and he assembled thirty thousand troops at Hamburg ready for an invasion to help them to make up their minds. The Danes, believing that the French would win the war against England, refused the English demand to hand over their fleet. England then forestalled the French, and invaded Denmark with an army of thirty thousand men.

The morning of the arrival of the English expedition at Elsinore, I had business in my line with a gentleman (Count Bernstorf's brother) whom I had been employed by for many years; in the dressing-room of Count F. I was engaged receiving his commands, when suddenly he turned his conversation on the English expedition that had arrived at Elsinore against the Northern Powers. His observations were of such a nature, that I turned to his lordship, saying, "I hope your lordship will pardon me if I do myself the honour of waiting on your lordship at some more favourable opportunity". I made my obeisance and withdrew. Thence I went on business with Mr. Drummond and Mr. Vansittart, whom I found in great confusion; they endeavoured to persuade me to quit Copenhagen with my family, as there was a ship at Elsinore to receive them, and I could go along with them, to England. I gave them to understand that that was impossible. These gentlemen had but a little time before being ordered by the Danish government to quit Copenhagen in four and twenty hours. They begged the favour of me to go and inform Mr. Rodenger, the Portuguese Chargé d'Affaires of their situation which I did with all speed. When I informed him, I perceived it threw him into great embarrassment; he took some papers under his coat and departed to Mr. Drummond's lodgings. On my return in hopes of giving further assistance, I found a mob of Danes assembled round the door in a very tumultuous manner; but I had the satisfaction to find that Mr. Drummond and Mr. Vansittart had taken their departure without injury.

I took every means of sending provisions to my country residence, which was called "Roolyetstal" (in English "Peaceful retirement") a very pretty place, about three-quarters of a mile from Copenhagen, and a small distance from the Sound between Denmark and Sweden; expecting the town would be besieged I laid in three month's provisions. The British armament came before the city on a Saturday, when on the Sunday I removed myself and family to my country house. My good friend Sir Levet Hanson dined with us for the last time. We had been acquainted in the most cordial manner for many years. On the Monday the English troops were lying on the ground before my house. Hand-bills were delivered to the inhabitants from the English, saying they were come as friends and not as enemies. My family and I were overjoyed at this pleasing declaration.

It being a most brilliant morning, the shipping and troops presented one of the finest sights ever seen. Placing confidence on the contents of the above mentioned hand-bills, I persuaded my wife and eldest daughter to take a view of the grand scene before our house. While walking we were alarmed at a soldier suddenly making his appearance, saying I must go with him, otherwise I should be shot; pointing at the same time to a horse soldier at the corner of the field. I leave the feelings of myself, my wife and daughter on this occasion, to the reflection of my readers, as it is impossible for me to describe the overwhelming misery this misfortune involved us in. The soldier who took charge of me conducted me to an officer whom I expected to find a gentleman, but this proved not to be the case. Being strongly guarded, I was sent to the brave lieutenant-general's quarters, where the troops were all under arms ready to meet the Danes, who came from the town in order to attack the British lines; a sergeant took me in charge and marched me down with the front line to repulse the Danish troops. In this situation, I was thinking of another world; my family, I thought, were in comfortable circumstances from my industry. When the action was over, I was marched back with the troops to General Grosvenor's quarters, where I was put under a guard of two sentinels at the door, without any kind of refreshment and had to lie on the bare floor all night. I recommended my family to providence, and slept till morning; when I awoke and found myself a prisoner. I saw through the window an officer come into the yard, whom I called to and begged to come to me. He did so, and I informed him of my situation; he said I had been quite forgot, as they were busy making out their returns; but he said he would let the General know of my situation. The General's servant came, and the guards at my door were dismissed, I was conducted to my breakfast, which of course was not a very agreeable one in such a place; but after this meal I found myself very much refreshed. Still my mind was very much oppressed from not knowing how to extricate myself, as I perceived I was still a prisoner. At length directions came for me to attend the commanding officers; when questioned by them I asked if they thought me a spy; adding, that I felt myself treated very ill, and begged them to let me join my family. Sir David Baird was at the head of the Military Board, he said he could not dismiss me, but that I must take a letter to Lord Cathcart, and accordingly sent me with a guard to headquarters.

When I arrived in Lord Cathcart's presence, and that of a number of officers, I presented Sir David's letter; after reading it his lordship asked me if my name was Sanders, which I answered in the affirmative; he then asked me to walk with him into the garden, putting his arm under mine as though I had been a most intimate acquaintance, to the astonishment of myself, and seemingly of all the numerous officers present. When we came into the garden, the weather being exceedingly warm, we walked under a large shady tree; his lordship then taking his arm from under mine, in a very deliberate manner took out his pocket book, and turning to me said he had been in Copenhagen, but in his map he had overlooked a piece of water that served the town; adding that he was of opinion I could inform him where this water was situated. I begged his lordship to desist from asking me any questions of such a nature; that I and my family had lived happily in that town upwards of twelve years; and I begged his lordship would let me return. Perceiving that I was indignant at his request, Lord Cathcart returned his pocket-book, and did not trouble me any more on that subject; he, however, informed me, that if he was to let me go back, the Danes would take my life, as I had been so long within the English lines. I acquiesced in his lordship's opinion. "I suppose, (said he), considering your situation in life you can find friends within the English lines who will receive you?" I answered "Most certainly, plenty". "Then, (added he), I will give you a pass to go anywhere you please within our lines, but if you attempt to cross to go home, you most certainly will be shot". His Lordship then gave me the pass, with strong injunctions to destroy it in case I should happen to be taken by the Danes. I thanked his Lordship for his advice, and politely took my leave for the present. Thence I walked about ten miles to a place called Droningore, the seat of Mr. De Conink, where I was kindly treated by the family, particularly by the two sons of that gentleman, as also my Mr. and Mrs. Chevalier, whose very kind treatment I shall ever greatfully remember.

My family's situation was a continual torment to me, it being impossible for us to hear a word from each other. I could have been much amused in my present situation if I had known their fate. My country residence, where I had left them, and which was called "Peaceful retirement", became the most noisy place, I believe, in all Europe, being the spot where most of the fighting and skirmishing took place near Copenhagen.

About a fortnight after my captivity, I took a walk to my old station, General Grosvenor's quarters, thinking to hear something of my family; but not an officer or anyone else could give me the least intelligence; they made every enquiry but in vain. I passed the whole afternoon with them very agreeably; on my way back to my friends I saw two sentinels at some distance from me, at the angle of the roads which led to different parts. I was proceeding when I heard the sentinel call out, and I thought he said "go back", much alarmed I was turning back, fortunately looked round and saw the sentinels taking aim at me; I then turned and walked towards them, and distinctly heard them say "advance". When I came up to them they demanded the countersign, of which I knew nothing. I was then taken under a guard to the next officer's quarters, where I was scrutinized and questioned through not knowing the countersign. At length I informed them I had a pass in my pocket, which I thought was sufficient protection. When I produced it, the officer said it was a pass from the Commander-in-Chief, but adding that it was a very great neglect not to give me the pass-word on my departure from the quarters I last left, as I was in the utmost danger of being shot by the sentinels. I found those officers complete gentlemen, they were exceedingly sorry they could not accommodate me comfortably. I spent some time very agreeably with them, and they said it would be dangerous for me to go forward, as the night was drawing on. I asked if they could send a guard with me to the opposite house, in which lived a farmer whom I very well knew, and who I believed would be glad to see and accommodate me. They called a guard, who happened to be the same sentinels who declared I should have been shot if I had not looked back at the time they first saw me. They conducted me safely to the farmer's house, where there was also a guard. I was received and made welcome by the husband and wife, and here I got to know the situation of my family, the female having been in the town a day or two previous. She informed me that my wife and children were arrested by the Danes, and put into the blue Tower, where they were safe, and all well. This was agreeable news to me. We had a fine dog, a most faithful creature, of whom we were all exceedingly fond, and it was a great grief to my wife and family that he was not allowed to be imprisoned with them; it was a wonderful thing, but the dog by some means or other found his way into the prison every morning and, when there, he would not eat anything until my family had all breakfasted. I shall relate something still more extraordinary of this dog hereafter.

I was also informed that all my friends had become my enemies, from the false report of a mean obsequious person, one Baron Sebby, one of a party of three, to whom, as I well knew, if the King had done the justice they deserved, he would have prevented the British hostilities, as they were the cause of the Danes breaking their neutrality: but to my own affairs.

A battle scene during the Napoleonic Wars. Note the large number of buttons on the mounted officer's uniform. Some button manufacturers received very large orders for buttons for military uniforms during these wars.

Chapter XII

Containing a description of the plundering German Legion, and Benjamin's brave rescue of the property of his friends while under fire.

An English foot soldier at the time of the English siege of Copenhagen, 1807.

Chapter XII.

I got all the news I could from the farmer's wife, and found myself more reconciled to circumstances. She accommodated me with what I greatly needed, a bed to rest on; being much fatigued, I laid down, and recommended myself and family to the mercy of the Creator of All Things and rose in the morning cheerful and much refreshed. I then walked to my friends at Droningore. The German Legion being quartered in those parts, I had a good opportunity of observing the nature of those miscreants; their cruelty and plunder on the poor people were past description. I got acquainted with some of the officers, whom I found as ferocious as the privates. So incensed did I become at their barbarity, that I was induced to go to Lord Cathcart's quarters, and make known their vile conduct; but was given to understand that the English Commander had no control over the German Legion, who belonged to Colonel Hoptimum.

I found my pass was much respected, and it protected me wherever I chose to go; I therefore had an opportunity of serving my friend Mr. Chevalier, he having a country house near the town in which he had left his family, out of the way of the siege. My friend was very unhappy in respect of his papers; his house was on an elevated spot, facing the Crown Battery, a very dangerous situation, and not a great way from my own house. I asked Mr. Chevalier in what places his papers and valuables were to be found. As my pass was so much respected I proposed to him that I should endeavour to get his papers, and I persuaded him to accede to my proposal; he gave me his keys, and I went with a man and a cart. I had to pass the German Legion by whom I was obstructed. I maintained my right of proceeding, which the officers denied, notwithstanding my pass. I then demanded to speak with the Colonel, which they could not refuse. When admitted, I asked him if I had the honour of seeing the Colonel; he said I had. I replied, I hoped he would excuse my begging to speak with him; he seemed a gentleman, therefore, I briefly informed him of what had occurred, and presented my pass. He then said I had liberty to pass where I pleased, and I never was obstructed afterwards. My man and cart, with myself proceeded to my friend's house, which I found occupied by about six

English officers, to whom I presented my pass, and acquainted them with the business I came upon. Losing no time I loaded the cart with all the papers and books I could. The bombs now began to fly from the Crown Battery, and I made the best of my way home to Droningore, to the great joy of the family.

I could not get all my friend's papers the first journey, I therefore, went the next day. Mrs. Chevalier gave me the keys of the wine cellars, requesting me to pass them to the officers in the house. I told those gentlemen that the lady of the house had sent them the keys of the wine, for them to use it, at their own discretion; they very politely begged me to present their compliments to the lady, and say that they returned the keys. How honourable this, and what a difference between our officers, and the murdering plunderers in the German Legion. I lost no time in collecting my friend's papers; the bombs began to fly from the Crown Battery, and I was here in great danger. One of them came very near me, knocked down a chimney, and then burst; a part of it struck a sergeant who was near me, at the back of his head so severely that his brain was exposed. He was taken into Mr. Chevalier's hot-house, and I was informed he breathed for six hours afterwards. I found three pieces of this bombshell in my friend's garden, which I put into the cart, thankful to the Almighty for my preservation. We returned in safety to my friend's at Droningore, who were all exceedingly anxious for my return; Mr. and Mrs. Chevalier could not express themselves grateful enough for the great services they said I had rendered them in preserving their papers and account books; it must have been a fatal loss if things had not turned out so favourable. Mr. Chevalier was in partnership with Mr. Duntzfelt, one of the first merchants in Copenhagen, their house, and that of Mr. Errickson's were the only two that withstood the shock; all the other mercantile establishments were ruined. In the course of the evening I introduced three pieces of bombshell, of which I made a present to the young De Coninks who expressed themselves very thankful, saying I could not have presented them with anything so acceptable, and that they would ever preserve them for my sake, and in rememberance of my achievements that day. I felt much gratified, and am confident I could not have served a more deserving family. I stayed with them till a flag of truce came by; I had only time allowed me to say I was alive and well, and no more, not even where I was; no further communication was allowed between myself and family. Being anxious to know their fate, I thought it would be better for me to get a lodging nearer headquarters; but I took my leave of them and of the most elegant domain in Denmark, and got lodgings at a village called Yentoft, eight miles nearer

Copenhagen.

I was now in view of all the proceedings against Copenhagen, which are exceedingly interesting; but I was kept in continual alarm, night and day, for the situation of my family, as the English operations were very much carried on against that part of the town where they were imprisoned. My time now was disagreeably spent chiefly among the German Legion, the greatest barbarians I ever saw; but my residence was convenient, as I could go every day to headquarters, and converse with gentlemen, as most of the English officers became acquainted with my situation.

One morning I heard a great noise among the officers of the German Legion; they were giving vent to the most ruffianly language against the English officers, who they said were feasting while they were starving. I went to headquarters, and informed them how I left those workers of misery; misery, I may well say, for my pen cannot describe the misery they occasioned the inhabitants wherever they went. When I returned from headquarters I found them in all their glory, drinking, eating and singing; they wanted me to partake with them, but I could not be persuaded and I always kept at a civil distance. They had broken into a gentleman's cellar, and found what was congenial to their vile propensities. Oh! what a life of wretchedness I led among those barbarians during a whole month.

Chapter XIII

In which he finds his house turned into stables, passes through enemy lines in disguise and recovers his family.

A night scene in Copenhagen before the British bombardment. Artist: J. Bundsen (1788).

The ruined city of Copenhagen after the British bombardment of 1807. The spire of St. Petri is in the centre. A woman is nursing her child in the ruins. Over 300 houses were destroyed and people are searching for their belongings in the rubble. Artist: I. M. Wagner.

Chapter XIII.

The British Army besieged Copenhagen for two weeks and began to bombard it on 2nd. September 1807. They bombarded it with hundreds of red hot shells and with Congreve's flaming rockets and soon set it ablaze. An English observer, crossing the Sound from Landskrona, found the night sky five miles away as bright as day, while his ship shook with the reverberation of the guns. The English bombardment lasted for three nights and then the Danes surrendered.

The bombardment and the capture of the Danish fleet was hailed as a great triumph in Britain, but it was attacked as a very high-handed act by the Whig opposition and by some of the Tory Government's supporters. Lord Sidmouth voiced the uneasiness of some Tories about Britain's ruthless action against Denmark, when he wrote, "We have done a deed, which will make our name hereafter quoted in competition with all the ill ones." But the government could plead that the extreme danger facing Britain justified extreme measures. William Cobbett agreed with the government, and stated strongly that if the Ministers did not deserve to be impeached for doing what they had done, they would have deserved impeachment for not doing it.

For Benjamin Sanders, the British invasion of Denmark meant financial ruin. His country house was destroyed by the British and the rest of his property was confiscated by the Danes. He and his family were forced to flee from Copenhagen in 1807, for no Englishman was safe there after the destruction of lives and property, and the extensive looting by the British forces and by the soldiers of the German Legion, who were foreign mercenaries in the pay of the English government.

At length, to my great joy, the Danes capitulated. I went to headquarters immediately I heard the news, and found it to be the fact. I then destroyed my pass and went to my country house; to my utter amazement I found my sweet place in a worse state than a wilderness. From hence I walked, in hopes of seeing my family in town; on my way I met two of my people; there being four gates to the town of Copenhagen, they told me there were two of them at each gate to prevent my going into the town, as in case I did, two Danes would surely murder me. They also informed me that my family were still prisoners in the Blue Tower. This was dreadful news to me; I had, therefore, no other resource than to return to Yentoft among the ruffianly German Legion. To my great mortification I stayed here three days longer, expecting every moment I should have some of my family come to me, but my hopes were vain. My anxiety got the better of me, and I was determined, let the consequence be what it might, to go into the town; but I fortunately bethought me it would be more prudent to go to headquarters first, and speak to Lord Cathcart, who was just sat down to dinner with General Waltersdorff. His Lordship came immediately to me, saying, "I am happy to inform you, Mr. Sanders, that your family are all well and at your house in town." He brought General Waltersdorff to confirm the good tidings, with which I was much pleased. I then made my thankful obeisance, and departed to my house in town, with joyful expectations of being happy with my family, again. When I reached it, however, I found it fast shut up, and sealed with ribbon across the door. I leave my readers to judge of my sudden affliction. When a little recovered, I went to a relation of my wife's who was much terrified to see me, and said if the Danes found me in town I should be immediately murdered; that there was a strict watch at the Blue Tower prison in hopes of laying hold of me. During the siege there had been the strangest falsehoods that could be circulated against me.

It is to be observed, that it was only the shipping and arsenal, not the town, the English were in possession of, which made my situation the more dangerous. What a dismal night I had in planning and contriving how to get to the English lines again. I disguised myself in a countryman's dress. Early in the morning I had two outposts to pass, and luckily I got by them unobserved. This was a very fortunate circumstance, for had either of the sentinels taken me I should have met with no quarter from the Danes; as it was I very cleverly got back to the British lines again. I was passing towards headquarters when I met a number of officers on horseback; though I was disguised they knew me, and all of them stopped, and I told them what had happened. A gentleman in the middle rose upon his stirrups, and said, "Sanders, make use of my name to Lord Cathcart, and tell him all you have told us; he will soon restore your family." I answered that I had not the honour of knowing the name of the gentleman who instructed me; I received an answer from him that his name was Grosvenor. I now continued my journey towards headquarters, and by the way met Lord Cathcart with his military attendants, whom I stopped, being well known among the gentlemen in the army. I informed them of the course of my disguise and of the unhappy situation I was in. His Lordship said he had intended going into the Danish arsenal, but instead of that he would now go into the town; he desired me to make myself easy, as I might depend on seeing my family very soon. To our unspeakable joy we soon all met in good health, and uninjured.

There now was an interval of six weeks before the departure of the English as stipulated in the capitulation. I lost no time in preparing for my departure for England with the fleet. I went to my country house, which had been a beautiful residence, but I found it in a state not to be imagined or described. Horses were in all my parlours, all the furniture was broken up to boil pots and kettles, not a bit of wood but what was torn away, and even the ground in my garden was taken to erect batteries against the town. I was much incensed at this horrible devastation of my lovely retreat, and determined to go to the Commander of the artillery. His quarters were at the Windmill Battery, where I found him at breakfast with another Officer; when introduced by his servant, I made my complaint, when he in a very rough manner said, "His Majesty's horses must have stabling." I replied there was stabling and a coach-house, without making use of my best rooms for that purpose. He was going to be very abusive, but the gentleman with him got up, saying, "General, I must say that the gentleman's premises have been most shamefully abused." The General then said, "Sir, I will give orders to Colonel Harding to investigate and make a report, and you will be sure to receive a suitable remuneration".

My property being destroyed by the English one way, and confiscated by the Danes the other, I became divested of all means of providing for myself and family; my only hope was in remuneration from the English Government. I shall state what that was in the succeeding narrative.

A little time before the siege of Copenhagen, we had information of my father's death; he lived to the advanced age of ninety-three. In his latter days he usually took a walk, and when he returned he slept a little before dinner; he was sleeping in his chair as usual on his last day, when the servant coming to wake him found him quite dead. About this time arrived intelligence of the death of Mrs. Smart, my wife's sister, with information that our former agreeable companion Mrs. Lindesay was gone to live with the eminent and worthy Dr. Sims, who was physician so many years to the family of the good Archdeacon Congreve.

I was now preparing to go with the English Fleet to England, with my wife and nine children; for this purpose I was recommended to Sir Samuel Hood, who behaved to me in a very gentlemanly manner, and appointed a passage for us on board the "Melbourn". I was necessitated to go, as the Danish became a military government; some of them were in my debt, particularly Luwenheim, one of the chamberlains to the King. My life was a terror to this worthy, as I once threatened to acquaint the King of his meanness and cowardice on a former occasion. It is well that we made up our minds to leave Denmark, as I was informed by my friends afterwards that I should have been sacrificed without mercy. When ready to depart, I went, by the desire of my wife and children to take leave of Mrs. Bearn, whom I have mentioned before; they now lived in a different part of the town. I found Mrs. Bearn in a room where there were five or six Danish military worthies, whom I looked at disdainfully, and politely walked up to Madame Bearn, informing her that in the name of my family I was come to take my last farewell; she got up and threw her arms round my neck, and kissed me in the most affectionate manner, in a flood of tears. On going, I looked at the military with a smile of contempt, shook my head at them, and departed. This interview was a great triumph, as these were the scoundrels that gave orders to the soldiers to shoot me if I came near my country house during the siege. Mr. and Mrs. Bearn were in the habit of living a little gay, which exposed them to such company as this. It happened that a conversation took place between Lord Cathcart and myself on a subject concerning the Danish Officers; I was by no means pleased, and it occasioned me to doubt whether his Lordship was altogether worthy of the title and honour he bore.

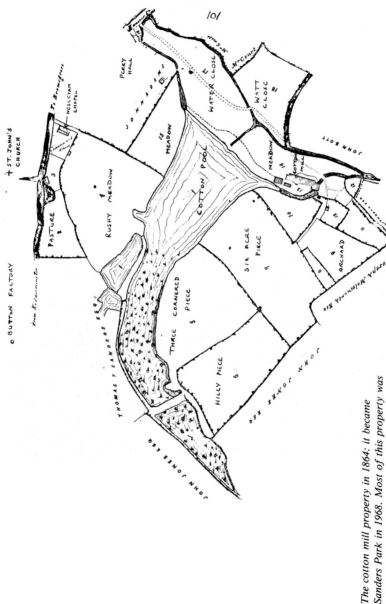

The cotton mill property in 1864: it became
Sanders Park in 1968. Most of this property was
left to the town of Bromsgrove by the two
granddaughters of B. Sanders in 1951.

Chapter XIV

In which he almost loses his wife and eight children in their tempestuous flight from Copenhagen and is found by his extraordinary dog in London.

Chapter XIV.

The day arriving for the fleet to depart, we had a boat to take our removables to the ship "Melbourn"; it turned out a most tempestuous day, and the boat, after going a very little way, began to let in water; we all thought we should soon perish but, fortunately a worthy captain, who saw our perilous position, sent his boat and took us and baggage out of the Danish boat into his own ship. Our grateful acknowledgments for this deliverance he received as a worthy man should. There was no time to be lost in looking after our ship. This good captain lent me a boat and one of my children went with me. The wind increased almost to a hurricane all that day, with much difficulty and anxiety we found the "Melbourn"; I and my little son John stayed on board her. Her captain sent a boat in company with the returning boat, to bring my family to the "Melbourn"; the wind seemed to increase and my anxiety cannot be expressed. At three o'clock in the afternoon of a dark stormy day at the latter end of October, all eyes looking anxiously out; at last the Captain said, "I see them all coming". My heart leaped with joy, but I heard him say the boat could not live to reach our ship, the weather made it impossible. It soon became almost dark; the Captain and his men cried out that they were all gone, and that they saw the boat go down. My distress now became insupportable. I took my poor little boy by the hand, and walked to the fore part of the ship, I was just taking him in my arms and about to plunge into the sea to put an end to my misery in this world. With my thoughts directed to the Supreme, just in the performance of this dreadful resolution, my attention was arrested by a voice crying out, "Is that the Melbourn", and up came the boat alongside, with my family all safe. What a dreadful situation for my wife, with eight children round her in an open boat on the sea in such tempestuous weather, and at such a time of night.

Early next morning we set sail, and had a tolerable passage, only that we were almost poisoned by Captain Jackson's neglect; his dirtiness and ill manners accorded very well, but were very disagreeable to us. This, however, was not of long duration; we made a tolerably quick run to Gravesend; from there we came to Billingsgate, and put up at the Gun Tavern until we got more convenient lodgings, which we soon did in Pickett Street, Temple Bar.

Soon after we arrived I had occasion to go into the City before breakfast; on my return we were sitting together, when in came my dog, whom we have often lamented. To see him come in with such expressions of joy and gladness was wonderful; he jumped and licked the children's faces, while we were amazed and overjoyed at his finding us out.

Benjamin Sander's extraordinary dog appears to have been left behind in Copenhagen during their tempestuous flight, and had followed them on another ship to the English coast and somehow managed to track them down to London.

Bromsgrove Button Factory today. (Originally Sidemoor Mill.)

Chapter XV

In which Benjamin finds himself in desperate financial plight because of the inhumanity of Lord Cathcart and of the government, and saves himself by inventing a new button.

Stamping Buttons (engraving of 1851).

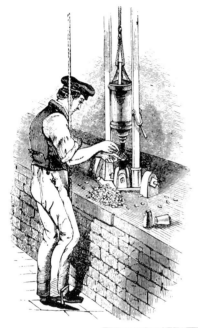

Little girls making buttons in a Birmingham workshop (from Chas. Knight's Cyclopaedia of Industry of All Nations *[1851])* (photo: Mansell Collection)

Chapter XV

Benjamin Sanders's failure to obtain any compensation from the British government for the destruction of his property is a sorry tale. Lord Cathcart, the commander of the English army in Denmark, treated Benjamin Sanders very shabbily and revealed a lack of humanity which completely belies Arthur Bryant's description of him as "a slow and kindly man." In contrast, General Grosvenor is shown as the only important figure who gave Benjamin Sanders any practical help. He used the money given to him by General Grosvenor to buy tools in order to make a new kind of button in a workshop in Lambeth, London.

After his frustrating experiences in trying to obtain justice from members of the government, it is not surprising that he viewed Mr. Bellingham, the murderer of the Prime Minister, Spencer Perceval, in 1812, with some sympathy. Bellingham shot the Prime Minister in the lobby of the House of Commons, and Benjamin Sanders believed that Bellingham, a bankrupt, had suffered in the same way as he had, at the hands of members of the government.

When peace was signed between Britain and France in 1815, Benjamin Sanders visited Copenhagen in an unsuccessful attempt to recover some of his property. He was clearly shocked by the poor state of Copenhagen and was not surprised to find that the Danes blamed Britain for the ruin of their kingdom and refused to compensate him until Britain made good Danish losses.

Between 1807 and 1813, driven by the necessity of rebuilding his fortune, Benjamin Sanders turned his inventive ability once more to the manufacture of buttons at Granby Place, Lambeth, ably assisted by his son Benjamin, who was a clever toolmaker. In 1813 Benjamin Sanders took out his first patent for a method of making cloth-covered buttons by machinery. This was the most important single invention in the button industry, leading to a much quicker production of cloth-covered buttons which were usually covered in silk. According to his patent of 1813, he used a series of metal cylinder dies for consolidating the various parts of the button. He also used presses or chargers to thrust the substances of which the button was made into the dies. Button-makers had been handicapped by the lack of efficient presses before Benjamin Sanders designed one. He also gave some flexibility to the metal shank of the button by interposing a spiral spring "between a small plate keyed or pinned through the shank behind the garment, and the garment itself." This patent of 1813 laid the foundation for the rebuilding of his fortune.

I had now to look to my finances, which did not amount to three hundred pounds; it appeared, therefore, useless for me to go into business. I was in hopes of the Government remuneration, but how to proceed I knew not. I was advised to see the Admiral who had the command of the fleet; I went accordingly to the Admiralty and acquainted him with my situation, and asked his advice. Surprised and disappointed, I soon found by his conversation he was a poor insinuating noodle; he persuaded me to tell a lie, of all things the most detestable to me. I left him not very respectfully, and never saw him more. I now heard that Lord Cathcart was arrived at an hotel in Pall Mall, and I took an opportunity of paying my respects to his Lordship; he was coming down stairs to his carriage at the time, and speaking severely to a servant concerning a lie the servant had told to him. When he had done he turned to me in a very kind manner, and inquired after my wife and children. I parted respectfully from his Lordship, much pleased with his kindness, thinking his Lordship would be of great service in applying for my remuneration. In two or three days after I did myself the honour of again waiting on his Lordship, who on this occasion was also coming down stairs. I begged him to put me in a way to recover my losses in Copenhagen; his Lordship hastened towards his carriage, I followed him but he quickly got in, drove off, and left me nothing but the rattling of his coach for my satisfaction. I could scarcely consider Lord Cathcart a gentleman possessed of principles of humanity; though I endeavoured to persuade myself that he must have recollected something of great importance which occasioned his immediate departure; I went home altogether in a dissatisfied state.

I was now much engaged in my button invention, which proved a very expensive undertaking, by no means suitable to my present situation. My inventions were all originals, therefore, I could not get any assistance but what I acquired by practice; by perseverance, however, I slowly improved in this particular article. Having been absent from England so many years, London seemed a new world to me, all my connection seemed to be dead and gone. I was passing through St. Paul's Churchyard one day, and met our worthy friend Dr. Sims, who expressed much pleasure at seeing me; my first enquiry of course was after our good friend Mrs. Lindesay, who the doctor told me was lately dead; he said she lived happily with him some years, at the latter end of his life; he had now retired from practising and was going to reside in Bath, where he would be happy to see us; we took a friendly leave of each other, and never met again.

My friend Sir Levet Hanson and I now opened a correspondence once more, to the great gratification of both. Sir Levet Hanson's letters to me will be seen at the end of this Memoir, and I trust will give much satisfaction. I had now a vast deal of trouble before me; I got a memorial drawn up, in expectation that Lord Cathcart would sign it; I was continually waiting on his Lordship, but never could have the honour of seeing him, which much perplexed me. I believe he went out of town, and took no notice of my memorial. I then wrote a short letter direct to the Earl of Liverpool at his office in Downing Street. A Mr. Bunbury brought me an answer that the Earl said my letter would be attended to. This message put me in great spirits, and I took a small house at Lambeth. After some time worn out with impatience, I wrote to the Earl again, giving my new address; I now waited a long time to no effect; my little stock of money was nearly expended, provisions were never known in England to be so extravagantly high; every week the prospect became more alarming. I, therefore, wrote again to the Earl telling him our situation and that I and all my family would come to his house on the next morning to implore his Lordship to provide something of a remuneration for my losses at Copenhagen. To this letter I received an answer, desiring me to come to Downing Street by four o'clock next day. This once more put us all in high spirits again. According to appointment I went to Downing Street, and was conducted to a room where there was a door opening into another, and a large round table placed in such a way that no one could see into any part of the inner room. Mr. Bunbury came in, and having seated me and himself exactly opposite the open door, began a conversation on the siege of Copenhagen; when I touched on my remuneration he always shifted from the subject, and my visit to Downing Street amounted to nothing, to our great disappointment.

I was now tired of playing the fool. Lord Cathcart came to town and put up at an hotel in Albemarle Street, where I waited on him, after I had sent him a fresh memorial for him to sign; but he did not sign it, neither would he see me. I wrote to his Lordship many letters, but received no answer to any one. I now began to be filled with indignation towards his Lordship, and wrote to him again requesting him to return me my memorial, but he would do neither one thing nor the other. For the last time I wrote to him in such terms that I afterwards wished I had not sent the letter. The waiter at the hotel informed me that his Lordship desired him, when I came, to tell me he was gone out. I could scarcely believe this but I put it so close to the waiter, that he said he would willingly take his oath on it. His Lordship's whole deceitful behaviour worked secretly upon me, being now very much reduced, so as scarcely to possess means of subsistence for my family, that I made up in my mind to watch an opportunity, not to assassinate his Lordship, but to knock him down, being driven almost to the extreme of self destruction. With this intent I went one evening to Albemarle Street, and saw Lord Cathcart's carriage at the door; the waiter told me his Lordship would soon be down. When I saw him descending the stairs I stood on the passage determined to put my resolution into practice; but his Lordship very luckily saw me, the passage being well lighted. He no sooner saw me than he called out, "Mr. Sanders", ran to me in the most affable manner, took me by the hand, and walked me quickly out of the passage into Albemarle Street, saying, "Sanders, what can I do for you?" I answered I trusted he would do what was necessary for me, as he knew well the situation of myself and family. We walked arm in arm together a good way up Bond Street, and his Lordship's conversation was very agreeable, he declaring on the word of a gentleman that he and General Grosvenor would do everything in their power to serve me; he also desired me to be sure to leave my address at his hotel. We had now almost got to his carriage, and seemingly a most cordial farewell took place. Oh! what a pleasure this was to me on my returning home. How thankful was I for so providential an escape. If my resolution had been executed, what misery it might have involved me in. Having waited about three days, I was now sure of having free access to his Lordship, but lo! when I came to the hotel, the waiter informed me he was on his way as Ambassador to Russia. I will now take the liberty of begging my readers to fancy themselves in my position for a moment. Oh! that mankind should come into the world with such inhuman feelings towards each other! But these reflections involve us in unfathomable mysteries, which on earth we cannot comprehend—they belong to Providence, who has provided that good shall come out of evil, as will be clearly seen in my succeeding narrative.

The word "Grosvenor" from his deceitful Lordship struck me. The reader will here recollect my captivity, and being taken prisoner to the quarters of General

Grosvenor. After my mind became calm, I sat down in good spirits, and wrote a narrative. I was very low in finances at this time. One morning I went with it to the General's house; I gave the servant a little note which he quickly took upstairs. I was immediately ordered up to the General, who with his lady and another gentleman were at breakfast. I politely approached the General saying, "General, your old prisoner takes the liberty of asking a favour of you, to sign this narrative." I was desired to be seated; the General read my narrative to all present, and I never shall forget the attention, and the compassionate looks cast on me by the lady. The narrative being read, the General rang the bell, gave orders for his writing things, and wrote under it as follows:— "This narrative of Benjamin Sanders is strictly true; I most sincerely and conscientiously recommend this case to his Majesty's Secretary of State." Signed "Grosvenor." The General gave me the memorial, and asked if that would do; I told him I thought it much more expressive than I expected; then he said, "Pray God, send it a favourable issue." I returned thanks, and made my obeisance to his lady, and the other gentleman present. The General waited on me to the door; on the landing I turned to make my last bow, and was going down stairs, when the General called me; I returned, he took me into his cabinet, and taking out of a drawer a Bank of England note of considerable amount, said, "Sanders, take this", I hesitated and drew back; then General Grosvenor came close to me and put his hand on my shoulder, saying in a low voice, "take it, when the Government have remunerated you, you can repay me." "Well, General (I said) on those conditions I will thankfully receive it." Here was a striking proof of the various dispositions of mankind. When we look round and observe the variety the Almighty has laid before us in the outer world, we cannot be surprised at the variety of dispositions in human nature. Here is a convincing proof that good comes out of evil; as Lord Cathcart's mentioning General Grosvenor's name at the time he deceived me himself, brought me a friend whom I found able and willing to receive me. I now became again a visitor in Downing Street, with more confidence than ever. The General's good work began to prosper, and his generosity was not bestowed in vain; my button business which had suffered for want of necessary tools, was now supported with spirit and we began to manufacture them fit for the market. Mr. Weston in Bond Street used them. I got acquainted with Mr. Weston by means of a servant of the Duke of Gloucester, who knew me as having done business for the Duke during his stay at Copenhagen.

Being anxious to know the result of my narrative signed by the General, I lost no time in begging the matter might come forward, but the delay was so long, that I began to think I had been playing the fool in Downing Street again, and I got weary of attending them. At last a young gentleman came to me from Mr. Bunbury, saying, "Your petition was returned by His Majesty in your favour, and is gone to the Treasury to be paid." This was good news indeed, and gave encouragement to our industry. After some anxious expectations I called one evening at the Treasury, where I saw Mr. Wharton, to whom I communicated my business; he said he knew nothing of it, and asked how I became informed of such a circumstance. I told him it was from Mr. Bunbury, in Downing Street, he then said, "Stop here a few minutes; I cannot recollect such a circumstance, but I will go and see." When he returned he said, "Yes, Sir, there is such a document in your name, Sanders, as you say, and you may depend you will hear from the next Privy Council." This was a little cheering; accordingly, as Mr. Wharton had told me, a letter came from the Lords of the Privy Council, expressing much sorrow that they could not accede to the request in my petition. I now determined never to play the fool in Downing Street again; we all bore the disappointment pretty well, and put more confidence in our industry. My Bromsgrove relation [James Wilkinson] and myself became again acquainted, and little family differences being reconciled, he proved to us a sincere friend.

The time now came that peace between England and France was concluded; my worthy friend Sir Levet Hanson left Stockholm for Copenhagen. I had transmitted bills to the house of Duntzfelt and Chevalier, whom I was in friendship with. This was the firm whose books and papers I preserved, mentioned at the time of the siege of Copenhagen. When I arrived in England I transmitted bills to the amount of eight hundred pounds. The severe restrictions laid on by the Danes prevented all intercourse with England, therefore, I never could get a remittance; but now, peace being at hand, and our friend Sir Levet Hanson being in Copenhagen, I, with my wife and one daughter, lost no time in going there to look after our property and visit our friend. When we arrived, Mr. Roll, Sir Levet's Secretary, gave us the mournful news of his death and burial the week before our arrival. His estate in Yorkshire fell to the son of Lady Collom, wife of Sir Thomas Collom. Here was a great loss as well as a great disappointment. I went to my friends, Messrs. Duntzfelt and Chevalier, and learned to my great mortification that my letters were opened by the Danish Government, and the contents confiscated. I had, therefore much property in the hands of the Government, and went to the good Count Jockim Bernstorff for advice, who kindly recommended me to the English minister, Mr. Forster; that gentleman took a great deal of trouble on my account, which I shall ever thank him for. I had various interviews with several head men in the Government, and lastly with Count Shimelman, a most worthy man, who said the English had ruined their Kingdom, and that when England had made good their losses, my claim would be settled, but if I would return with my family, nothing would be wanting. We found Copenhagen deserted, and all the great mercantile houses become bankrupt, except the house of Duntzfelt and Chevalier my friends. It gave me great pleasure that I had preserved their books and papers. This trip to Copenhagen at the cost of a twelve month's time, turned out a mere Downing Street business. When I called on Count Bernstorff, he had he said been a long time out of office, but now he was going with the King to meet the sovereigns of the Holy Alliance; he, however, took a polite farewell of "Benjamin the Rooter", as the Count and his brothers were pleased to call me in happier times.

We now soon took leave of what friends we had, arrived in England again and found all my family in good health, and business going on well. Previous to my late voyage to Copenhagen I engaged myself in co-partnership with a person of property in Dublin, who purchased a patent for my new invented buttons for the United Kingdom, I preserving my English patent to myself. My good son Benjamin was to go with me to conduct the concern, he being exceedingly ingenious at making what was requisite for executing the business. When I left Dublin it was with regret, on account of my son, for I had seen something in my partner that did not please me, but I had confidence in my son that he would not be corrupted by immoral example. When I returned from Copenhagen, my anxious desire was to see my son, and to be acquainted how the business answered; my partner had been continually before pressing me to let him have an equal share in the English patent, till at length I insisted that he should never mention anything more on that subject. He had provided in our articles of agreement that he should have the whole and sole management of the business, my son's share of it excepted. I was soon informed of his unfair practices, and called him to arbitration, and after a vast deal of trouble I agreed to give him the Irish patent, and thank Heaven got rid of him. Being now left entirely to our own resources, unshackled by the Downing Street, and Copenhagen affairs, we applied ourselves to business with ingenuity and industry.

About this time Mr. Perceval was shot, an event which gave me a great shock, as I conceived that Bellingham's case was similar to my own. Goaded as I was by the wilful deception of Lord Cathcart, thank God I never had any idea of deadly weapons, but I was wound up to a thorough feeling that his Lordship justly merited chastisement at my hands. If that nobleman should ever look over my narrative he may feel assured I owe him no ill will. I would at the same time recommend to gentlemen who fill high offices of state to pay some regard to poor men's solicitations for their rights, and not suffer them to get exasperated by losing their time to no purpose. It is a false notion that mere promises will get rid of complaints; for suffering men when they find themselves deceived rouse themselves to resentment, yield to despair, and are at last driven to a state of insanity. In this state men are crafty, and one individual has immense means of mischief in his power, if inclined to be revengeful. I certainly think I shall be excused if my feelings have been warmly expressed. When my petition was so substantially signed and sealed by the generous General Grosvenor, consider the fate it met, as I have already stated; consider the behaviour of Lord Cathcart, and my interview with the hypocritical Admiral; when I explained to him my business, "Be sure (said he) if the Government ask you if you were a Burgher of Copenhagen not to let them know that you were." This was persuasion to tell a lie, which I ever considered a most heinous crime mean and despicable in any man. Look at my situation with so large a family, the gentlemen in Downing Street lifting me up to certainty as it appeared, and at last deceiving and throwing me down into a gulf of misery; am I not justified in saying they were a barbarous cold blooded set of men?

Bromsgrove High Street looking south in 1840. The three houses which Benjamin Sanders inherited in 1821 are in the left foreground, adjoining each other, next to the Hop Pole Inn. One of the houses has the sign of Mr. Brown, plumber, on its front (now Brighton's Shoe Shop). Benjamin Sanders's first button manufactory in Bromsgrove was in the workshop at the rear of this house. The houses are numbered 52, 50 and 48 and are still standing.

Chapter XVI

In which he invents an improved button in Bromsgrove and establishes his large Button Factory.

Benjamin Sanders's Button Factory at Sidemoor, Bromsgrove. It employed 300 people by the 1830's, mainly women.

Top: Photo c. 1890. Benjamin Sanders extended the Factory in 1829 from the point of the slightly raised crest of the roof on the right of the chimney. It was burnt down in 1915 leaving one small part of the original late eighteenth century mill. Middle photo.

Benjamin Sanders's first small button factory in Bromsgrove. It was the workshop behind No. 50 High Street (now Brighton's shoe shop) which he inherited in 1821. It is now occupied by a pottery studio, 'Wattle and Daub' and is reached from Windsor Street.

Chapter XVI.

I will now speak only of matters more pleasing to my feelings. We all united and put our abilities in motion; and with the blessing of Heaven, soon reaped the fruits of our industry. We removed from London to Birmingham for the purpose of greater convenience. We now were thirteen miles from Bromsgrove, where my friend and relation lived, and we had the pleasure of seeing each other conveniently; he was a gentleman of a genteel independence, a most excellent well behaved man; but he became aflicted with the disorder which terminated his life soon after we arrived in Birmingham. He left me all his property except a few legacies, which bequest was the occasion of our settling at Bromsgrove.

We had now carried on business about fifteen years, the same length of time as had elapsed from the commencement of my business in America to the end of my stay in Copenhagen; a time of profitable industry all lost and my property consumed, and with it the Danish nation ruined. Being known in the English army so well at that time, and having frequent conversations with officers of good understanding, I never met with one who did not condemn such destruction as most unjustifiable. The property the English armament took from the Danes, besides the fleet, was immense. There was one ship of the line on the stocks; this also fell a sacrifice, she was cut into four parts, broken up and left in the dockyard, the most dismal sight that can be imagined. This last act was condemned as most unprincipled, and a disgrace to the English administration of the time.

Being occasionally acquainted with the happiness and prosperity of my American farmer and his numerous family, and of those whom I settled at Albany, has occasioned us the most heartfelt satisfaction.

I now bring my narrative to a conclusion. My readers, I trust, will be gratified to be informed that after so many dangers and troubles, and many of a minor nature which I have not mentioned, my wife and self have now arrived to the verge of seventy years of age, we have been near fifty years together, with all the mutual love and respect that the events of our lives required, which I believe has proceeded mainly from the good disposition of my partner. I had often promised myself the pleasure of writing this narrative, if ever I should be so happy as to arrive to a state of independence. The arm of the Almightly has seemed to protect me throughout, and I have the happiness to look back on life well spent, and not spent in vain. I have been lately in London, principally engaged in writing the preceding pages, in the hope of giving satisfaction to my friends; what I have written are facts, on which the reader may place the most implicit confidence. We now finally return to our friends for the kind and liberal treatment they have shown us, and in requital we most sincerely wish them to enjoy as many years of happiness as we have done. They may be assured it will add to our satisfaction to receive them at our pretty place "The Cottage" of Bromsgrove, where they will find us surrounded with one of the happiest families in England.

Benjamin Sanders's signed guarantee for his customers in France, warning them about imitations of his buttons.

This guarantee indicates that many of his buttons were exported.

Translation:

**In order to avoid imitations,
purchasers are advised to
demand for each gross of our
buttons, besides the former ticket
carrying our name in full letters,
our signature as below.
Signed in Bromsgrove,
14th February 1842.**

Benjamin Sanders's button factory at Sidemoor, Bromsgrove. It employed
300 people by the 1830's, mainly women.

The button factory and its much smaller workforce in 1892. On the extreme
right the last of the Sanders family to run the factory, Mr. H. Sanders of Lion
House. Next to him is Mr. J. C. Nicholls who managed the factory at the very
youthful age of 17 years. The fourth person from the right is Sarah Nicholls,
J. C. Nicholls's grandmother, who was forewoman. The sixth figure from the
right is Joe Porter who worked the big presses making big buttons, together
with the eighth figure from the right, Mr. William Guest. The lady in between
the two men is Mrs. Guest, the sister of Sarah Nicholls. The man on the extreme
left is Mr. H. E. Eborall, toolmaker.

Benjamin Sanders moved to Birmingham, the centre of buttonmaking
in about 1820. Birmingham had become the greatest buttonmaking town
in Britain during the eighteenth century, particularly because of the
growing popularity of metal buttons. By the 1770's, there were more
people making buttons in Birmingham than any other article, and one
hundred and four firms were listed as manufacturers of buttons in a
directory of 1773. Southey described Birmingham in the early nineteenth
century:

"The noise of Birmingham is beyond description; the hammers
seem never to be at rest. The filth is sickening: filthy as some of our
own old towns may be, their dirt is inoffensive; it lies in idle heaps,
which annoy none but those who walk within the little reach of their
effluvia. But here it is active and moving, a living principle of mischief,
which fills the whole atmosphere and penetrates every where, spotting
and staining every thing, and getting into the pores and nostrils. I
feel as if my throat wanted sweeping like an English chimney. Think

not, however, that I am insensible to the wonders of the place:— in no other age or country was there ever so astonishing a display of human ingenuity: but watch-chains, necklaces, and bracelets, buttons, buckles, and snuff-boxes, are dearly purchased at the expense of health and morality; and if it be considered how large a proportion of that ingenuity is employed in making what is hurtful as well as what is useless, it must be confessed that human reason has more cause at present for humiliation than for triumph at Birmingham.''

Benjamin Sanders moved his button manufactory from Birmingham to Bromsgrove in 1821, when he inherited three houses in Bromsgrove's High Street from his cousin James Wilkinson, a prosperous linen and woollen draper. These houses adjoined each other next to the old Hop Pole Inn and are still standing, numbered 48, 50 (now Brighton's shoe shop) and 52. Benjamin Sanders began manufacturing buttons in the workshop behind No. 50, which is now a pottery studio with its front in Windsor Street. His son Thomas Sanders, a button manufacturer, was living at No. 52 in 1841, and he inherited the three houses on the death of Benjamin Sanders.

He probably bought the larger Sidemoor Mill for his Button Factory within a short time of moving to Bromsgrove, because the demand for his cloth-covered buttons was so great. Sidemoor Mill was a disused cotton spinning mill when Benjamin Sanders bought it; John Collett had inherited the mill from his father Richard Collett and had spun linen yarns there, employing about eighty people until his bankruptcy in 1810. In an indenture, dated 1808, in the possession of John Nicholls, Sidemoor Mill was described as a mill with a steam engine, and a buckhouse with a bleaching ground next to it. The mill which Benjamin Sanders bought in the 1820's was clearly one of the first spinning factories in the country and one of the first to use a steam engine.

When Benjamin Sanders lived in Bromsgrove, it was dominated, like Birmingham, by the noise of hammers, wielded by hundreds of nailers in their nailshops attached to their small houses. Dugdale described Bromsgrove in 1819 as ''a large and dirty place, full of shops and manufacturers of needles and nails, sheeting and other coarse linen''. The population of Bromsgrove parish was seven thousand five hundred in 1821, but only half of these people lived in the town itself. The town was also dominated by the needs of the coaching trade, with up to thirty-two coaches a day passing along its turnpike roads.

Within four years of moving to Bromsgrove, Benjamin Sanders took out his second patent for the manufacture of cloth-covered buttons. This was a major improvement on his first patent, because a flexible, soft shank replaced the metal shank on his buttons. He introduced a piece of canvas which protruded through the back of the button, and through which a needle could pass freely. These buttons could be more easily and more neatly sewn on to garments, than those with metal shanks. These improved flexible buttons took the market by storm and in 1829, Benjamin Sanders had to extend his Button Factory in Willow Road to cope with the growing demand. Sanders's buttons became the fashion and tailors received orders that no other buttons were to be used. The photograph of the Button Factory shows the extension of 1829 from the point where the roof is slightly raised on the right hand side of the picture. The Button Factory then became the biggest factory in Bromsgrove employing about three hundred people, mainly women, in the 1830's and 1840's. It remained the biggest factory until the Railway Freight Waggon Factory was built at Aston Fields in the 1840's.

New ideas were quickly copied in the button industry and in 1831, Mr. Aston, a Birmingham button maker, was making copies of Benjamin Sanders's flexible shanked buttons. Benjamin Sanders brought an action for infringement of his patent against Mr. Aston, but the action was lost unfortunately, owing to a technical fault in the way his claim had been phrased.

In the same year, Benjamin Sanders faced a major challenge from Benjamin Aingworth of Birmingham, who also took out a patent for making cloth-covered buttons. Aingworth's invention was an improvement on Benjamin Sanders's buttons, because the backs of his buttons were almost entirely covered with fabric (silkbacks), which could be used for sewing the buttons to the garment. There was no projecting tuft on his buttons, so they did not wear out button holes so quickly. On account of the keen competition in the making of cloth-covered buttons, Benjamin Sanders bought Aingworth's patent at the very high price of a three hundred pound annuity to Aingworth. Despite the price, it proved to be a wise decision, as it enabled the Bromsgrove Button Factory to stay ahead of its competitors for some years. By the time of Benjamin Sanders's death in 1852, however, many manufacturers had copied the Sanders patents in Britain and abroad. There was also a general decline in Birmingham's button industries in the 1850's and 1860's, mainly because of foreign competition and loss of exports, but also because of the changes in fashion.

Demand for Sanders's buttons slumped, until by 1860 the Bromsgrove Button Factory employed less than a quarter of the three hundred workers which it had employed in the 1840's.

It was said that Benjamin Sanders made £40,000 by his use of Aingworth's patent alone. This figure has to be multiplied at least one hundred times in order to estimate its value in today's money. Unlike many inventors, Benjamin Sanders made a large fortune, and he invested most of the profits from his Button Factory in land and property in Worcestershire, Herefordshire, Warwickshire and Middlesex. His most extraordinary achievement was in becoming a multi-millionaire, despite having been financially ruined at the age of forty-five. The surprising extent of his property is detailed in his will made in 1845 and proved in 1852. He owned seventeen town houses, including four in Bromsgrove, three in Stratford-on-Avon, one in Droitwich and nine in London. He was the lord of two manors in Herefordshire, the manor of Street and the manor of Hinton (otherwise Harton), and also the owner of eight farms with their numerous cottages. This property was divided between his four surviving sons and two daughters.

Levett Sanders inherited the house built by his father in Bromsgrove, the 'Cottage', the piece of land next to it called Moor Furlong, a farm at Shepley, in Bromsgrove, the mansion of Street Court, Street Court Farm and Shire Woods in Herefordshire. John Sanders inherited three houses in Stratford-on-Avon and a farm in Martin Hussingtree with several cottages and the sum of £5,000. James Sanders inherited Munderfield farm, the manor of Hinton, Hinton farm in Herefordshire and a house in Droitwich. Thomas Sanders inherited three houses in Bromsgrove High Street, land in Sidemoor, Bromsgrove, Porch House Farm and Torn Hill Farm in Herefordshire, a third farm in the parish of Dormstone and the sum of £3,000. His daughter Amelia inherited a piece of land, nine houses and four coach houses in Ebury Street and Burton Street in London. Finally Benjamin Sanders left £5,000 to his married daughter, Mrs. Elizabeth Rodway. The spring from which this fortune flowed, the Button Factory and the land adjoining it was left to Benjamin Sanders's four sons as tenants in common. The full extent of Benjamin Sanders's wealth is not completely given above, however, for he had already shared some of his property between his children before making his will. For example, he owned Brickhouse Farm and 60 acres of land in the parish of Stoke Prior which he had given to his son James Sanders. Rarely has such a large fortune grown out of the manufacture of so small an object as a button.

Diary of Events 1763 – 1984.

1763 Benjamin Sanders born in Worcester.

1775 B. Sanders apprenticed to Mr. Lingham, draper in Worcester.

1775 The American War of Independence began with the Battle of Bunker Hill.

1782 B. Sanders became a tailor in London.

1789 The French Revolution began.

1790 (approx.) B. Sanders invented his 'ventilator' for men's breeches.

1792 B. Sanders sailed to America. He began making buttons in New York.

1793 Start of the war between Britain and revolutionary France.

1794 Yellow fever epidemic in New York. B. Sanders almost died.

1794 B. Sanders started a tannery in Laminburg.

1795 B. Sanders left America and sailed to Denmark. He started a tailoring business and a silk manufactory in Copenhagen.

1795 – 1802 Napoleon's rise to supreme power in France.

1801 Battle of Copenhagen — Nelson defeated the Danish fleet.

1807 Siege and bombardment of Copenhagen by British army. B. Sanders lost his fortune and returned to London.

1812 Spencer Perceval, the British Prime Minister was assassinated.

1813 B. Sanders's first patent for the manufacture of cloth-covered buttons.

1820 (approx.) B. Sanders moved to Birmingham.

1821 B. Sanders moved to Bromsgrove and started his Button Factory.

1825 B. Sanders took out his second patent for the manufacture of cloth-covered buttons with a soft, flexible shank.

1829 B. Sanders extended the Button Factory. (300 employees).

1831 B. Sanders bought Aingworth's patent.

1840 B. Sanders II died — eldest son of B. Sanders.

1852 B. and P. Sanders buried in St. John's churchyard.

1870 George Nicholls became the manager of B. Sanders & Co.

1875 G. Nicholls became a partner in the firm.

1880 G. Nicholls introduced the "Excelsior" button.

1882 B. Sanders & Co. acquired Chatwin and Sons of Birmingham, specialists in thin buttons covered with gutta percha.

1890 George Nicholls died and his son J.C. Nicholls joined the firm.

1900 J.C. Nicholls introduced buttons made from velvet, satin, silk and braid.

1912 The firm began to make celluloid buttons on a large scale.

1915 A fire destroyed the Factory.

1923 The firm purchased a casein button business from Mr. Cole of Birmingham.

1924 The firm purchased the Worcester Button Company from Weintraud & Co., Ltd. of London.

1927 John H. Nicholls joined the firm.

1928 The plant of the Worcester Button Co. was transferred to Bromsgrove to begin the manufacture of leather buttons.

1929 The firm started to make chromium-plated buttons.

1935 The firm started to make injection-moulded buttons.

1958 Another fire; only one small part of the original Sidemoor Mill remained.

1982 David Nicholls joined the firm.

1984 John H. Nicholls and his son were still manufacturing under the name of B. Sanders (Bromsgrove) Ltd. until October 1984. The firm then passed to the control of Alan Jones of Fattorini & Son, Ltd., who is, however, keeping B. Sanders in the firm's name.

Chapter XVII

An account of his descendants and their mark on Bromsgrove.

Sanders Park.

Copenhagen Cottage built by Benjamin Sanders.

Steps House. Georgian home of B. H. Sanders the Town Clerk.

B. H. Sanders. Town Clerk, 1860 – 1910. Grandson of Benjamin Sanders.

Chapter XVII.

The descendants of Benjamin Sanders I continued to make their mark on Bromsgrove. Benjamin Sanders's eldest son, also named Benjamin, inherited his father's inventive ability and contributed a great deal, as a tool-maker, to his father's inventions; he died in 1840 aged forty-four. Benjamin Sanders I's grandson, Benjamin Hadley Sanders, a solicitor, became a leading figure in Bromsgrove, when he was Clerk to the Local Board (Town Clerk) for half a century, between 1860 and 1910. He and his family, consisting of two unmarried daughters, Miss Lucy Sanders and Miss Mary Beatrice Sanders, lived in the fine Georgian house which is still standing next to St. John's Church, called "Steps House" and later at "Oakdene" on the Kidderminster Road. He had a firm way of dealing with obstreperous councillors and was involved in some bitter rows over proposed developments in the town.

In 1900 one of these disputes between B.H. Sanders and a minority of the town's councillors was reported in some detail in the "Bromsgrove Messenger". The Town Council was sharply divided about the purchase of a site for a Market Hall, some supporting the purchase of one site and some another. The Chairman of the Council and Councillor A.B. Crane led a minority group of councillors who opposed a resolution of the majority to purchase the "Roundabout House", next to the Town Hall, for the proposed Market Hall. They accused B.H. Sanders of being influenced by the councillors who supported the purchase of this site and of hastening the process of the purchase because of the mounting opposition in the town to the scheme. The following extract from the newspaper report gives some of the flavour of the heated exchanges between B.H. Sanders and his critics, and how he kept full control of the situation, stressing that as Town Clerk he was the legal servant of the council, but not their menial servant. At one point he remembered the tailoring background of his grandfather, when he rounded on the Chairman of the Council meeting, and told him that he would have to jump into twenty pairs of breeches before he could frighten him.

The Clerk : You were told you were not in order.

Mr. Crane dissented.

The Clerk : You are telling a lie, sir.

Mr. Crane : Half a minute, and I will show you you are telling one. (Some confusion.)

The Clerk : I hope the Chairman will conduct the meeting properly or I shall appeal to the other members.

Mr. Crane : You are a servant.

The Chairman : I must rise. (To the Clerk :) You impute to me improper motives, and I have not spoken. I do not care for your bombast. I will not have it.

The Clerk : Do not talk to me. Get out, sir. You will not frighten me. You will have to jump into twenty pairs of breeches first.

The Chairman : I say you have no right to speak to me in that way.

The Clerk : He told a lie and you did not call him to order.

Mr. Crane : I will prove it.

The Chairman : At a meeting when Mr. Fitch was chairman you said when the Chairman asked you you would speak. You have not been appealed to. If you wish to make a few remarks, do so without getting in an awful temper.

Several members spoke and

The Chairman said : After this unseemly scene I will vacate the chair, and the meeting will be at an end.

The meeting was, however, continued.

The Clerk was about to speak, when Mr. Crane, who remained standing, said : Sit still until I have finished. You are a servant.

The Clerk : Not a menial servant.

Mr. Crane : Stand on your legs the same as members of the Council.

The Clerk : It is not the position of the clerk to "stand on his legs." I do not want a man like you to teach me my duty. I should be sorry to take a lesson from you on etiquette, manners, morals, or anything else.

Mr. Crane : Nor should I from you.

The Clerk : A lie is implied in the second case and expressed in the first case, and you had better be careful how you act, or you may stand before twelve more of your countrymen on your " rock."

Part of Benjamin Sanders's fortune was invested in more land and property in and around Bromsgrove after his death, especially along both sides of the Kidderminster Road; in 1853, one of Benjamin Sanders's sons, James Wilkinson Sanders, bought the Cotton Pool property, which included Watt Close Mill and Cotton Mill Pool, and thirty-seven acres of land adjoining it along the Kidderminster Road, from Frederick Winn Knight. The plan of the property is given below. Watt Close Mill had been a water corn mill until the late eighteenth century, when it became one of the first cotton spinning factories in England. Much of this Cotton Pool property was left to the town by B.H. Sanders's two unmarried daughters, Miss Lucy and Miss Mary Beatrice. They both lived to a ripe old age, dying in 1945 and 1951 respectively; Miss Mary Beatrice was 94 years of age when she died. When Miss Lucy died she left seven fields adjoining Chestnut Walk, off the Kidderminster Road to the town, and her sister confirmed this gift in her will. Benjamin Sanders's button fortune thus created Sanders Park for the enjoyment of the people of Bromsgrove.

Thomas Tudor Sanders, became the owner of the Cotton Pool property in 1864, when the Cotton Pool covered an area of nine acres. He had the Pool drained in July 1865, much to the disappointment of most of the youth in the town, who had learned to fish, skate and play ice hockey on it. The Cotton Pool was drained through a large lock, through which the Battlefield Brook ran eastwards. According to Dr. George Fletcher, who witnessed the event, an enormous number of fish came tumbling through the lock on to a large grating, during the three days which it took the pool to drain. The reclaimed land then became fertile market gardens. B.H. Sanders had the old Cotton Mill demolished in 1892 and he made an open air swimming bath on the site, the only swimming bath in the town until after World War II. Bromsgrove Fair, held annually on the 24th June, the day of the patron saint of the parish Church, St. John, was held on the large meadow called Watt Close in the mid-nineteenth century, and probably for many years previously.

There is other tangible evidence of the Sanders family in the town. The fine house which Benjamin Sanders built on the Kidderminster Road, close to his Button Factory, which he called "Copenhagen Cottage" or the "Cottage" is still standing. It was called "Denmark House" by a later owner. The Victorian house, known as "Oakdene", Kidderminster Road, where Miss Lucy Sanders and her sister lived for many years, and where both of them died, is also still there.

The Sanders family gave generously towards the restoration of St. John's Church in 1858. B.H. Sanders was a member of the Restoration Committee and Miss Maria Sanders was the first to respond to the vicar's appeal for money for the restoration, when she headed the subscription list with the sum of one hundred pounds in 1857. She also gave the brass lecturn to the Church in 1862. Miss Maria Sanders lived in one of the finest Georgian houses in the High Street; this is now a shop, No. 67. At her death she had an expensive, old fashioned funeral, with mutes standing on each side of the door, each one holding a long black wand with a large bunch of crepe tied at the top. They remained there during the whole day of the funeral.

More surprisingly, part of Benjamin Sanders's Button Factory remains in Willow Road, Bromsgrove and is still trading under his name, B. Sanders & Sons (Bromsgrove) Ltd. A bad fire destroyed a large part of the original Button Factory in 1915 and, unfortunately, destroyed the business records of the firm. John Nicholls and his son continued to manufacture buttons and badges there until 1984; badges were a natural extension to the button business. Four generations of the Nicholls family have run the Button Factory, starting with George Nicholls, who became manager of the firm in 1870.

When George Nicholls took over as manager of the Button Factory, the girl employees were paid one shilling and one penny per day, and his wife, as forewoman, received ten shillings a week. This was one penny a day more than the girls could have obtained from many other jobs in the town. George Nicholls was manager during the difficult period of the Great Victorian Depression (1873 – 1896), when the button industry, like many others, suffered from declining demand and prices actually fell. In 1890 the Bromsgrove Button Factory was making buttons at prices twenty-five per cent below the prices it had obtained thirty years earlier. Only 26 women and three men were employed by the firm in the 1890's, and the men made the large buttons, which required the use of some heat in the manufacturing process.

Millions of Bromsgrove buttons have gone round the world since 1821, when B. Sanders established his Button Factory in Bromsgrove. At the present day it employs between fifty to sixty people. The old industries of Bromsgrove, the making of salt, leather, bricks, cloth, nails, needles, bells, carriages and waggons have faded away, and button making is now the oldest industry in the town. Benjamin Sanders's Button Factory has also a wider claim to fame: not only is it the oldest business left in Bromsgrove, it is the oldest cloth-covered button business in the world. The first factory for the production of cloth-covered buttons was not established in America until about 1833 by Samuel Williston in Massachusetts.

Charles Dickens, in his "Household Words" summed up the

attraction of buttons and the spirit of Benjamin Sanders, when he wrote, "There is surely something charming in seeing the smallest thing done so thoroughly, as if to remind the careless that whatever is worth doing is worth doing well."